COMPETING WITH
THE RETAIL GIANTS

National Retail Federation Series

COMPETING WITH THE RETAIL GIANTS:

How to Survive in the New Retail Landscape

KENNETH E. STONE

WILEY

John Wiley & Sons, Inc.
New York • Chichester • Brisbane • Toronto • Singapore

ISBN 0-471-05440-2 (cloth).—ISBN 0-471-05442-9 (paper).

Printed in the United States of America

10 9 8 7 6 5 4 3 2

ACKNOWLEDGMENTS

I would like to thank my wife, Janis, for her support, not only during the writing of this book, but in my other endeavors over the last 30 years. I would also like to express my appreciation for the encouragement offered by our two sons, Eric and James. In particular, James was of great assistance to me in conducting library research, in constructing my illustrations, and in doing some of the copy editing. Lastly, I would like to thank Robert Watson of Iowa State University Library, for his valuable library research during the early stages of the manuscript.

TABLE OF CONTENTS

PREFACE

I didn't plan to go down the road that I am now on. I didn't plan to become an "expert" on competing with mass merchandisers, or to travel the world presenting seminars, or to write a book on competing with the mass merchandisers. I didn't spend a penny promoting myself. In fact, it all happened by word of mouth. As a friend once said, "this thing has taken on a life of its own." It all began when I conducted a study on the impacts of Wal-Mart stores on Iowa towns.

Many people ask me, "How did you get started doing these studies?" The answer is fairly simple: it's a part of my job. In addition to being a professor of economics, my primary job is as an extension economist. That means that I extend the university to the business people of the State of Iowa. Shortly after I came to Iowa State University in 1976, I developed a program called *Retail Trade Analysis*, using the excellent sales tax data available. The State of Iowa publishes an annual report of the sales of all towns and cities in the state, based on sales tax collections. For communities with a population above 2,500, the sales are also reported by merchandise category.

The retail trade analysis consists of two parts. Part 1 uses the sales tax data to illustrate the trends in sales for the subject town for the last several years and compares its sales patterns to those of the surrounding competing towns. Part 2 analyzes the current situation for the subject town and examines each merchandise category to determine if it is above or below average for towns of a similar size. In effect, the retail trade analysis checks the economic health of a town's retail sector and is the equivalent of a physical examination for a person. Just as with a physical exam, sometimes townspeople think their town's retail sector is abnormal, but after seeing the retail trade analysis they realize that, in fact, it is quite normal. Conversely, sometimes townspeople believe that their town's retail sector is above average, but find that it is actually below average in certain aspects.

The retail trade analysis program has been quite popular and many communities have one conducted every year to use as a barometer of their progress. Furthermore, the state's Department of Economic Development requires that communities have a recent retail trade analysis in their portfolio before they can be certified in the Community Economic Preparedness Program.

The outstanding sales tax data has also allowed me to perform other applied studies. For example, in the late 1970s I conducted a study for the 1980 White House Conference on Small Business, where I documented the migration of retail sales from rural counties in the Midwest to the urban counties. In the early 1980s I used the data to conduct a study of the impact of shopping malls on Iowa host towns and surrounding towns. This study received considerable national attention and was one of the first of its kind.

In the mid 1980s, I started receiving calls from Iowa merchants and chamber of commerce executives where Wal-Mart had just announced that they were building a new store. Typically, I was asked to come to their town, help them ascertain the likely impacts of a new Wal-Mart store, and determine what actions they could take. By 1988 I had considerable sales tax data for a sizable sample of towns, over a long enough period to conduct a study on the impacts of Wal-Mart stores in Iowa. Although I had nothing against the company, it was becoming clear that their stores were having an impact on other businesses in their trade area. Many people have asked me, "Why Wal-Mart? Why didn't you study Kmart or Target? Again the answer is simple: Wal-Mart was the only company that was undergoing significant expansion. The other companies built very few stores during this period. Therefore, Wal-Mart was like a "living laboratory" that lent itself to easy and meaningful study. By the end of 1988, I had completed the first study on the impacts of Wal-Mart stores in Iowa.

At about the time I was finishing my 1988 study, the *Dallas Morning News* in Dallas, Texas, was running a series called The Wal-Marting of Texas. One of their reporters found out about my study and quoted me in his article. Shortly thereafter, another reporter from another newspaper called about the study. By the time I had conducted the 1989 study, I was getting an average of one call a week from reporters and one a week from business people.

I started receiving invitations from Iowa communities that were about to become host to a new Wal-Mart store to present my findings. However, it quickly became apparent that the study results alone would not satisfy local merchants. They wanted to know "What do we do about it?" Because of their requests, I developed a set of strategies to help local merchants coexist in a Wal-Mart environment. The strategies were derived from my several years' experience working with independent merchants.

By 1990, I was getting an average of one call a day on the subject and was starting to get invitations to travel outside the state to make presentations. By 1994, when Wal-Mart announced that it had purchased 122 Woolco stores in Canada from the Woolworth Company, I received 20 to 30 calls per day on this subject from Canada and throughout the United States. To date, I have presented seminars in 49 states, in most of the Canadian provinces and in Mexico. I have recently received invitations to speak in places as far away as Australia.

My work is especially worthwhile when I receive a letter or phone call from someone who has attended a seminar and they tell me their business has improved after they implemented a few of my recommendations. I always remind retailers that both the largest companies and the smallest businesses on main street can get into ruts and just plain forget the basics of doing good business, and that's what gets them into trouble. I encourage participants to go home and re-think how they are doing business. I urge them to reinstate some of these basic principles and put the *quality* back into their businesses.

After reading this book, you too will re-think how you are doing business, and hopefully make a commitment to bringing my strategies to your company. Your customers will appreciate it; your employees will appreciate it; and you will have the self-satisfaction of knowing that your company is among the best.

PART I

ASSESSING YOUR COMPETITION

1

INTRODUCTION

To say that retailing in the United States has changed more in the last six to eight years than it changed in the previous three decades is a strong statement, but when one considers what has happened during this period, it is clear that the changes have been monumental. This book is intended to help independent business people and small chain store operators compete more effectively in a retail environment that by the day is becoming increasingly competitive. In Part I, this text assesses the characteristics of the stores which have, in part, influenced this trend. Part II will show you how to work alongside the large retailers, in order to capitalize, rather than lose out on, their presence.

GROWTH OF THE DISCOUNT MASS MERCHANDISERS

Over the past six to eight years, there has been a great proliferation of discount general merchandise stores such as Wal-Mart, Kmart, and Target and a great increase in regional discount general merchandisers such as Venture, Shopko, Ames, and so on. There has also been a rapid increase in the number of membership

3

warehouse clubs such as Sam's, Pace, Price, Cosco and BJ's. These are generally austere stores operating on a very thin profit margin handling a limited selection of merchandise.

"Category killer" stores such as Home Depot, Builder's Square, Home Quarters and Lowe's are also increasing at a rapid rate in the building materials area. In consumer electronics, firms such as Circuit City and Best Buy are taking an ever bigger share of the market. In toys, Toys "R" Us has become a dominant toy seller. In books, stores such as Barnes and Noble and Crown have carved out a respectable share of the market. In office supplies, Office Max, Office Depot and others are changing the way people buy office supplies. And there seems to be no end to the number of stores that lend themselves to "category killer" stores as proven by recent entries into the pet supply business such as PetSmart and PetStuff.

Factory outlet malls are also popping up all over the country. They usually have an interesting mix of name brand stores handling various soft goods and hard goods; are often built in a modular fashion so that it is easy to add more stores when feasible; and are usually located on interstate highways several miles from metropolitan areas. These factory outlets have the potential for competing with local merchants handling the same merchandise. Therefore, it is important to locate the malls outside the trade area of local merchants to avoid the perception of predatory marketing against some of the companys' own dealers.

Factory outlet malls depend heavily on attracting impulse traffic from the heavily traveled highways, but they are also strategically placed within the commuting shed of metropolitan areas from which destination shoppers are drawn. But, it appears that the better known factory outlet malls also attract people from other states who plan shopping trips in conjunction with their travel through the area.

The merchandise sold at the factory outlet malls are usually "firsts", but some of the stores sell irregular or "seconds" merchandise. Some of the fashion stores use the outlet malls as a way of closing out the previous season's styles. Still other hard line stores sell reconditioned merchandise through the outlets.

Specialty mail order has been growing rapidly in the last few years also. There are now a huge number of relatively small firms that offer fairly narrow lines of merchandise targeted at select or "niche" audiences. In most cases, catalogs are sent to consumers in the niche groups on a regular basis. Toll free telephone calls are the most common way of placing orders for this merchandise. Most of the catalog companies offer some form of expedited delivery (sometimes overnight) so that customers can receive the merchandise quickly. Specialty mail order appeals to many people who have difficulty finding the specialty products in retail stores. It also appeals to very busy people who have little time in which to do their shopping. The presence of discount mass merchandisers has clearly:

1. caused market saturation;
2. driven retail prices lower;
3. given consumers many more choices;

and consequently has made it more difficult for small businesses to operate profitably.

ANALYZING MARKET SHARE

It is difficult to obtain precise numbers on the sales of all retail stores. This stems from the fact that many are sole proprietorships and there is no official accounting of their sales. However, some idea of the rate of growth of the discount store industry compared to all retail stores can be seen in the bar graphs in Figure 1-1. The total retail industry excluding automobiles is illustrated in the top set of bars for 1991 and 1992. Reported sales for discount retailers are shown in the set of bars at the bottom of the figure. The important point is that *total retail sales* grew at a 4.5% rate from 1991 to 1992, whereas the growth for the known *discount retailers* grew at a 15.5% rate during the same time period. These figures are from *Discount Store News*, and substantiate the assertion that discount stores are a major factor in the rapid change in retailing.

Figure 1-1 Discounters Capture Larger Share of Retail Market

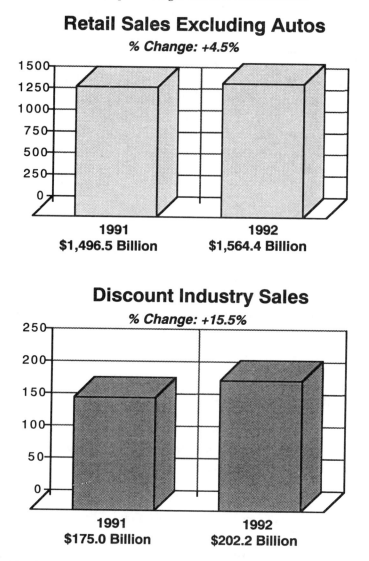

Retail Sales Excluding Autos
% Change: +4.5%

1991	1992
$1,496.5 Billion	**$1,564.4 Billion**

Discount Industry Sales
% Change: +15.5%

1991	1992
$175.0 Billion	**$202.2 Billion**

Source: DSN/U.S. Census Dept.

Figure 1-2 is a pie chart showing in greater detail the market shares of various discount formats in 1993, as a percent of all public mass merchandisers (not total retail). This illustration indicates

Figure 1-2 Mass Discounters Dominate Retail

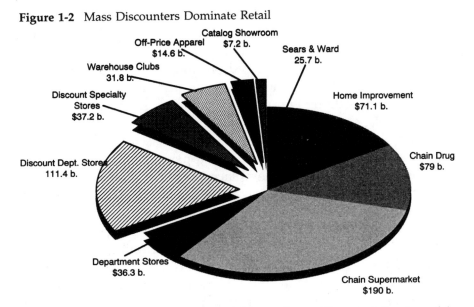

Source: Discount Store News, National Home Center News (retail sales only), Drug Store News, Food Marketing Institute, Business Guides, Inc./CSG Information Services

that the sales of discounters ($202.2 billion) account for about one-third of all mass merchandise sales. Total mass merchandiser sales ($602.3 billion) made up about 36% of all retail sales (excluding automobiles) in 1993.

PUTTING QUALITY BACK INTO RETAILING

In order to succeed in a mass merchandising environment, the local merchants and smaller chains must instill quality into their retailing and service operations. The word *quality*, as used here, does not necessarily refer to handling better quality merchandise. Instead, it means doing everything in the business with an emphasis on quality. It means hiring good people and giving them quality training. It means adopting new technology and methods to become more efficient. It means operating a clean and "user-friendly" store. It means displaying merchandise in a logical and attractive manner. It means incorporating attractive signage to inform customers of the benefits and features of certain products. It means developing variable pricing, where price-sensitive merchandise is competitively priced. It means having a modern returns policy that is in line with what customers have come to expect. It means doing everything right the first time.

Parallels can be drawn with some of the manufacturing sectors in the United States. The automobile sector is perhaps the best known example of what can happen when quality is de-emphasized either through complacency or through the desire to make more short-term profits.

For years, American automobile manufacturers dominated the market. They offered a quality product at a competitive price and were the envy of the world. However, beginning in the 1970s, more and more Americans began considering some of the smaller import cars from Europe and, in particular, from Japan. The smaller cars met their needs for greater fuel efficiency during the OPEC oil embargo episodes, when the supply of fuel declined and the prices sky-rocketed. As more Americans drove these small fuel-efficient cars, they also began to recognize that they offered better quality and reliability than some of the American cars they had been driving.

Meanwhile, American automobile manufacturers seemed to take the attitude of "build it and they will buy it." As a result of this, and the "if it sells, don't fix it" attitude, there was little team work or communication between engineering, marketing, production, purchasing, etc. The companies were slow to introduce more fuel efficient designs, and seemed to be more concerned with how fast they could run the assembly lines rather than whether the cars were being assembled properly. Production line workers had no authority to stop the assembly line to correct a deficiency as did Japanese workers. Consequently, American cars were given a quick check as they came off the assembly line. Those that had obvious deficiencies were shunted to the side where teams of workers would replace or repair the deficient items. Most people would realize that it is much easier—and more economical—to correct deficiencies during assembly rather than after the fact.

The sad truth was that many deficiencies in American cars were not detected until customers found them, often on their way home from the dealership! It was quite common for purchasers to keep a "bug list" in those days (1970s and early 1980s), where all the deficiencies were noted, in hopes that they would be corrected on return trips to the dealer's service department. This did nothing to foster loyalty toward American car brands.

In the early 1980s, American car companies began to realize that they needed to make major changes in the way they designed, manufactured, serviced, and sold automobiles or they would be displaced by foreign manufacturers. To their credit, the "Big Three" auto companies (General Motors, Ford, and Chrysler) have made monumental improvements in the ways their companies operate and the end result is that they are now producing better cars of a higher quality. Customers are coming back and market share has increased!

Small retail merchants and small chains do not have the resources of Chrysler, Ford or General Motors, but they do have the ability to improve the way they run their businesses. In truth, many of the qualities needed to improve a retail store can be done with limited resources. It doesn't cost anything to greet customers with a smile. It doesn't cost much to put up better signage. It doesn't cost anything to learn how to handle an irate customer with tact. It doesn't cost much to do something extra for customers, like carrying packages to their cars.

Some of the things necessary to improve quality, like adding a new scanner checkout, might cost money in the short run, but will pay huge dividends in the long run. Adopting a more liberal returns policy might also appear to be a cost, but in the long run it keeps customers coming back and therefore pays long-term dividends.

More than anything else, the management and employees of a retail store must make a commitment to improving quality. Doing things right the first time must become the everyday goal of every worker in the business. This means that you do not sell a garment with a stain or a defect to a customer, without first fixing it. It means that you do not send a customer off with a new set of tires with a cross-threaded lug nut. It means that you check over mechanical things before the customer takes them home to make sure everything is okay. It also means that you always send a customer away with a thank you and a smile. The bottom line is, that you can "out service" the larger stores with just a little ingenuity.

Building a quality organization means that a company can never "rest on its laurels". Continually looking for ways to improve is an essential element to improving quality. This practice is one of the ways in which the top retailers such as Wal-Mart and Home Depot remain competitive. Store employees, called "associates," are encouraged to find better ways and are rewarded when they do.

Entire books have been written on the subject of benchmarking. This book does not discuss the subject at length, but gives enough detail to instruct most merchants on how to successfully carry out the process.

ATTITUDE TOWARD COMPETITION

The attitudes of owners and managers of independent stores and small chains are very important in determining their success or failure in competing with the discount mass merchandisers. Merchants all over North America are faced with competition from new discounters entering their market. The range of emotions and attitudes expressed by these people varies from outright panic and despair to outright complacency. The distraught people often make remarks such as, "I think I will sell my business immediately." Conversely, the complacent people will make remarks such as, "I'm not worried about this new discounter coming on the scene; store 'Y' came in 10 years ago and it did not bother me.' Neither of these attitudes is adaptive when a large national mass merchandiser is about to enter the market area. Existing merchants should be somewhere in the middle. Certainly, the coming of a large discounter is not the end of the world, but it is a significant event.

Existing merchants should recognize the positives: the mass merchandiser will probably enlarge the trade area and generate a lot of traffic. The trick is to learn how to tap into that traffic without going head-to-head with the discounter on the same merchandise. There is no question that it can be done. There are successful small merchants all across the country who have learned how to "play the game" and have found ways to co-exist and, in fact, thrive in the presence of mass merchandisers. The merchants who worry me the most are the ones who say, "I've been doing business like this for 25 years. I don't see why I need to change now." As was stated earlier, retailing today is changing faster than ever before. The merchants who do not change with it are probably not destined to be in business for much longer.

MAKING THE COMMITMENT TO IMPROVE

To improve your store's operation, you will need to make a commitment to bring your quality up to that of the best in the field. In industry the term "benchmarking" is commonly used. Benchmarking is a method for determining important characteristics in a business and then finding the companies that do them the best. The goal of your company is to become as good as or better than these companies in every way possible. For example, when Ford Motor Company set out to design the original Taurus, they benchmarked many other cars for dozens of features believed to be important to consumers. In other words, they looked for the cars that had the best features they were seeking. They intended for the Taurus to meet or exceed the best of these various features found.

Retailers can make the same type of quality commitment by investigating the competition. When Sam Walton was alive, he was always shopping his toughest competition to see what they did better than Wal-Mart. He would then find a way to make Wal-Mart stores as good—or better—than the competition in such features. Sam Walton was a master at "benchmarking." This book tells you how to contend with the mass merchandisers by using some of the best-known tactics for improving quality and service, so that you may complete with the "master" at his own game.

2

THE RAPIDLY CHANGING
RETAIL ENVIRONMENT

Has retailing in the United States changed more in the last decade
than it had in the three previous decades, combined? That is a hard
proposition to prove, especially when considering that the three
previous decades could be characterized as a period of shopping
mall development across the country. Malls were powerful attrac-
tants and fundamentally changed shopping patterns—causing
shoppers to abandon downtown shopping areas in large numbers
and shop in the malls (usually in suburban areas) which offered
controlled climate, plenty of free parking, gigantic anchor stores,
lots of specialty stores and convenient shopping hours, all under
one roof. Most downtowns in the United States did not respond in
any meaningful way: many left parking meters in place; continued
to close at 5:00 p.m. or 5:30 p.m.; continued to allow store workers
to park in front of the store; and, in general, had very little
coordination or cooperation in establishing policies or promoting
downtown shopping. Downtowns are losing their former function
as central community shopping areas and meeting places, and

have evolved to a blend of service type businesses such as real estate offices, lawyers, accountants, and insurance agencies, along with a dwindling mix of retailers.

In the last decade we have seen the rapid growth of several formats generally characterized as *discount mass merchandisers.* The categories are:

1. Discount general merchandisers
2. Membership warehouse clubs
3. "Category killer" stores
4. Factory outlet malls
5. Specialty mail order houses

The operational methods of these formats will be described, and the operations of a few of the larger companies will be discussed in detail.

DISCOUNT GENERAL MERCHANDISERS

Discount general merchandisers encompass such national chains as Wal-Mart, Kmart and Target, as well as several regional chains such as Ames, Caldor, Bradlees, Hills, Venture, Shopko, Roses and more. They range in size from 30,000 square feet to 140,000 square feet, depending on the age of the store and the size of the market area. These stores typically have 30 or more departments and relatively low prices due to a lower level of service than traditional department stores, and also due to continual improvement of operational efficiency. They usually carry between 40,000 to 80,000 stock keeping units (sku's), that is, separate items of merchandise.

A typical discount general merchandise store would include most of the following departments:

- Ladies' apparel
- Men's apparel
- Boys' apparel
- Girls' apparel

- Infants' and toddlers' apparel and supplies
- Shoes
- Fashion accessories
- Jewelry
- Consumer electronics
- Greeting cards
- Books and magazines
- Hosiery
- Home furnishings and decorations
- Household products and cleaners
- Hardware and paint
- Candy and food
- Draperies and bedding
- Health and beauty aids
- Cosmetics
- Housewares and appliances
- Office supplies
- Fabric and crafts
- Automotive parts and supplies
- Sporting goods
- Toys and games
- Pet supplies
- Lawn and garden center
- Auto service
- Snack bar
- Luggage
- Paper products
- Vision center
- Photo service/portrait studio
- Cameras
- Video tapes, audio tapes, compact discs
- Furniture/picture frames
- Pharmacy
- Layaway

A discussion of some of the companies follows. The bulk of the discussion is about Wal-Mart because it is, by far, the largest and fastest growing retailer in the world.

Wal-Mart

The Beginning

Sam Walton and his brother James L. (Bud) Walton began operating variety stores in Arkansas after World War II and, by 1960, had become the largest Ben Franklin franchisees in the country. Ben Franklin was a national chain of variety stores, sometimes known as five and dime stores. At about this time, Sam Walton began hearing about some of the early discount stores operating in the eastern part of the United States such as Ann & Hope, Two Guys, and Zayre. He made several trips to inspect these stores and apparently liked what he saw. Then Herb Gibson started Gibson Discount Stores in Texas. Sam noticed that most of these stores were located in larger cities, and he wondered if the same concept might work in the smaller towns in the South where he was having considerable success with variety stores.

Once Sam Walton decided to get into the discount store business, he had a hard time getting anyone else interested in providing financial support. He first went to Ben Franklin and asked for their support, but they were not interested. He tried Herb Gibson and others to no avail. His brother, Bud, and his first store manager bought into the first store at about 5% of the total needed. Finally, Sam and his wife Helen decided to borrow the remaining 95% by mortgaging nearly everything they owned. They had decided to build the first discount store in Rogers, Arkansas, a town near Bentonville, AR, their home and the home office of their small variety store chain. Since there was already a Ben Franklin store in Rogers, Sam caused quite a stir among the Ben Franklin people since he would be going head to head with one of their stores. The store opened in July, 1962. Coincidentally, that is the same year that Kmart and Target began operation.

The Early Years

Wal-Mart grew slowly in the early years. By 1970 Sam Walton's "empire" consisted of 18 Wal-Mart discount stores and 14 Ben Franklin stores generating around $44 million in that year. By this time company debt was mounting and money was becoming tight. In October of 1970, the company went public and shortly thereafter sold off the Ben Franklin stores. By 1980 the company had grown to 276 stores generating $1.2 billion in 11 southern and midwestern states.

1980 to the Present

The 1980s and early 1990s were a spectacular growth period for the Wal-Mart Company. Sales increased from $1.2 billion in fiscal year 1980 to $67.3 billion in fiscal year 1994 which ended January 31, 1994. Annual sales for this period are shown in Figure 2-1. The number of Wal-Mart stores grew from 276 stores in 1980 to 1,953 stores in 1994. The number of Wal-Mart stores by state is shown on the map in Figure 2-2. The cities in which Wal-Mart stores are located can be found in Appendix 1.

Strategies

For the first 25 years of its existence, Wal-Mart's locational strategy was to establish stores only in relatively small- to mid-size towns. The idea was to build a dominant size store in the smaller towns and thereby capture a substantial share of the local market. The concept worked, verifying the premise that people really do not want to leave their own town to shop in another town; they only do so when they feel they do not have reasonable alternatives in their home town. Sam Walton gave small town residents reasonable alternatives and they stayed home in droves. In addition, the Wal-Mart stores attracted a large number of customers from the surrounding smaller towns, many of which did not have a critical mass of retailers needed to hold the local residents. In the late 1980s Wal-Mart enlarged its locational strategy to include the suburban areas of larger cities, thereby engaging in tough competition with larger and better known retailers than it had encountered in the small towns.

In addition to its small town locational strategy, Wal-Mart's other major strategy was to sell at "everyday low prices." To the casual observer this seems like a subtle difference between Wal-Mart and its major competitors like Kmart, Target and its many other regional competitors. Virtually all the competitors offered customers a sale a week. They produced weekly circulars that came to be known as "sales flyers." These circulars were usually

Figure 2-1 Wal-Mart Net Sales

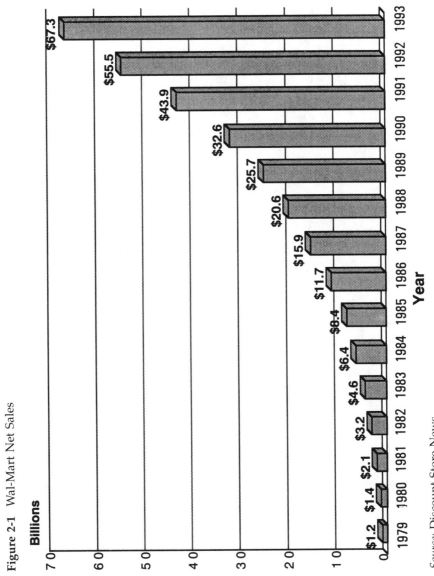

Source: Discount Store News

Figure 2-2 Number of Wal-Mart Stores by State

Source: Wal-Mart Annual Report, 1994

inserted in local newspapers or free advertisers for shoppers. Sometimes they were circulated via the mail. Most customers came to view the merchandise featured in these circulars as being "on sale." In addition, many people came to believe that the thousands of other items in the store were perhaps not all that great a value. There have been other problems with the weekly circular system. Often, certain items illustrated in the circular were not available in the store or were a different model or style than the items on the shelf. This meant that correctional advertisements had to be run to notify customers. If a popular item was advertised, it was quickly sold out and the store usually offered the later customer a "rain check," which seemed to disappear down a "black hole," never to be heard from again. Add to these problems, the embarrassment of reaching the cashier with what you believed to be a sale item, only to find that the model you selected was not, in fact, on sale, and many customers started preferring to go to a place like Wal-Mart where they came to believe that everything was lower priced everyday. In fact, it is virtually impossible to be lower priced than all competitors everyday, but Wal-Mart offered the ultimate caveat, by establishing a policy that they would meet any competitor's price if you found one to be lower than theirs. Today, most of Wal-Mart's competitors continue to produce weekly circulars, but in addition, they too are claiming to have everyday low prices and also offer to meet any competitor's lower price. It remains to be seen how customers will respond to this new approach.

Adoption of Technology and Concepts

The adoption of new technology and concepts is one of the main reasons that Wal-Mart has been able to grow rapidly while reducing operating expenses as a percent of sales. In 1990 Wal-Mart edged ahead of Kmart and Sears Roebuck to become the largest retailer in the United States. By the end of calendar year 1993, the company's sales had pulled ahead of Kmart and Sears by approximately $33 billion.

Wal-Mart has always been an experimenter with new technology and concepts. It will try new ideas in a few stores on a test basis. When the company finds a concept that does not work, they drop it. For example, a few years ago, they experimented with large recycling bins at the edge of their parking lots where customers could dispose of recyclable materials such as newspapers, aluminum cans and plastic and glass containers. At first glance, one assumes that customers loved having the bins handy at a place where they frequently shopped. However, it quickly became apparent that many people abused the service by dumping all manner of junk into the bins, often to overflowing, thereby causing an unsightly mess and disrupting parking lot traffic flow. Whether for these reasons or for others, Wal-Mart has taken these bins out of most of their parking lots.

On the other hand, Wal-Mart started experimenting with point of sale (POS) scanner checkout in 1981. At that time, supermarkets were the primary businesses using scanner checkout. Company officials quickly recognized that scanner checkout had great potential for increasing the company's efficiency and for speeding customers through the checkout line. For example, scanner checkout offered salary savings by eliminating the need to place a price sticker on each item. More importantly, however, the scanner system offered the potential for great improvements in inventory control. Every time an item was dragged across the scanner, inventory levels would be reduced accordingly and reorder levels quickly detected. Wal-Mart adopted the POS scanner checkout throughout its system by 1984.

However, for this information to be of maximum value, it had to be transmitted quickly to distribution centers, buyers and towns ultimately to vendors. At this time most of Wal-Mart's stores were located in relatively small towns in the South and Midwest. In the early 1980s many of these small towns did not have state-of-the-art telephone systems. In other words, the systems were not capable of transmitting the volume of data that Wal-Mart was generating through its POS scanner system. Whether it was for this reason or because of a visionary look at the needs of the future, the company decided to acquire and deploy a communications satellite system that became fully operational in 1987. The system provided two-way data and voice transmission capability and one-way video broadcast capability from headquarters to the stores and distribution centers. Shortly thereafter, the system was enhanced by adding a credit card authorization system that secured authorizations within five to seven seconds, a considerable time savings over the older systems that transmitted over public phone lines.

The company further demonstrated its enthusiasm for sophisticated technology by controlling the heating, cooling and lighting for most of its stores from one central headquarters location. To some this might seem like too rigid a centralized control, but it guarantees optimal operating conditions for stores without the constant attention of store personnel, thereby freeing them up for more meaningful and productive activities. Once while on an escorted tour of a new Wal-Mart store in Pennsylvania, the manager told me that he had just had a call from headquarters informing him that he had a hot spot in his storage room, but not to worry, the thermostat would be turned down to the proper level by headquarters personnel. The manager is freed up from some of the normal "putting out of fires" associated with store operations, and can turn to more positive, proactive functions.

Distribution System

Wal-Mart has one of the most efficient distribution systems in the world: one of the main factors that gave Wal-Mart a big advantage over its competitors. At the time the company was started, Sam Walton was apparently worried about the reliability of merchandise distributors and trucking companies. He was concerned that they could not get merchandise from the manufacturer to the store in a timely and efficient manner. He liked Ben Franklin's distribution center system and patterned Wal-Mart's first distribution center in Bentonville, Arkansas after it. The idea was to ship as much merchandise as possible directly from factories to the chain's distribution center, and then to ship directly from the distribution center to the stores.

The distribution centers were the focal points for store expansion. Stores were built in a circular fashion around each distribution center until its capacity was reached. Then another distribution center would be built some distance away and the process would begin all over again. It is for this reason that Wal-Mart seldom jumped over one state to get to another. They wanted to fill in the voids systematically.

As time went on, the distribution centers became more automated and more sophisticated. Today's distribution centers are as large as 1.2 million square feet, a space so big that nearly 27 American football fields could be placed inside. Not only are they large, but they employ the latest in state-of-the-art materials handling and inventory control. They employ cross-docking techniques whereby much of the merchandise coming in from the factory works its way through the building and ends up at the opposite end of the center on trucks going to the stores, without ever being stacked on the shelves.

Wal-Mart requires that virtually everything it purchases be UPC bar-coded. Trucks from the factories back up at the dozens of doors at the receiving end of the center. The cartons are unloaded onto high speed conveyer belts which run past a series of laser beams that read the bar codes. Eventually merchandise required for particular stores reaches the other end of the center where dozens of trucks are waiting to be loaded. Nearby high volume stores usually get a delivery each day. A store can run out of something one day and have it back in stock the next day with minimal human intervention. This is made possible because of the highly sophisticated tracking and distribution system that bar-coding allows.

Does this quick response distribution system really make a difference at the store level? At the very least, it keeps Wal-Mart's out-of-stock situations to a minimum. Frequent replenishment of stock can "make or break" a sale. For example, I own a private brand lawn mower found only at certain hardware stores. Last spring when I was doing a tune-up on the mower, I decided I needed a new air filter. I went to the hardware store to purchase it, but they were out of stock. I then went to the local Wal-Mart store, but they too were out of stock. The next day I went through the same routine. I went first to the hardware store, but they were still out of stock. I then went to the Wal-Mart store and they had a new shipment already on the display rack. I needed the filter badly and you can guess where I purchased it.

Control of Shrinkage

Shrinkage is the difference between what the records indicate is in stock versus what a physical inventory shows to actually be in stock. A small amount of shrinkage is attributed to breakage or improper handling. But the majority of shrinkage is attributable to shoplifting both by customers and employees. If not controlled, shrinkage can eat up a company's profits. Conversely, by tightly controlling shrinkage, net profits can be increased. Wal-Mart takes several measures to control shrinkage. The ceilings of their stores are laced with surveillance cameras that can scan the entire store. Perhaps more importantly, the company has a pact with its associates. If they work together to keep shrinkage below a certain targeted level, each associate will be rewarded with a check at end of the year reflecting the success of their efforts.

Benefits Plan

Wal-Mart has an attractive benefits package for their full time associates. In particular their stock purchase plan has allowed their long-time associates to accumulate wealth far beyond their cohorts working for other retail companies. There have been several stories written in trade journals about long-term employees who own Wal-Mart stock worth several hundred thousand dollars. How can Wal-Mart maintain happy dedicated associates with their rather ordinary wage scale? It's easy to be happy working for $6 or $7 per hour if you know that you are accumulating above average wealth in the stock market.

The profit sharing plan is also an important benefit. It's much easier to maintain dedicated and motivated workers when they know that if they work hard, they will benefit at the end of the year if profits go beyond a targeted amount.

Customer Service

Many people perceive that they receive a higher level of service in a Wal-Mart store than in some competing stores. Much of this is by design. Most Wal-Mart stores stock merchandise during the day, even though it would be more economical to stock at night when there would be a minimum of interruptions. I believe this is done to maintain a presence in the aisles. There is always someone around with a blue Wal-Mart smock, of whom you can ask questions. Furthermore, some store managers train their stockers to take the initiative and greet customers as they come down the aisle and ask if they can help them find anything. This is more than one normally expects from a discount store, and one feels that one is receiving a higher level of service. This is a relatively inexpensive way to maintain repeat customers.

It was recently reported in a trade journal that Kmart was going to start stocking at night, on the recommendation of a consultant who claimed that they would save 8% in stocking fees by making the change. This is probably a short-term saving. In the longer run, when customers cannot find anyone to help them and they start shopping elsewhere, how much are the savings then? This may be another case of a company taking the short-term, rather than the long-term, view.

Wal-Mart associates are also taught not to point in the direction of a department when they are asked where items are. They are taught to personally lead the customer to the items and point out the selection. Last year while doing some comparison price shopping in a North Carolina town, my host and I entered a competitor's store directly across the street from a Wal-Mart store. I asked where the incandescent light bulbs were located. The young employee at the front of the store said she wasn't sure, but she pointed vaguely to the rear corner of the store saying she believed they were in that general direction. It took my host and I another 10 to 15 minutes to find the bulbs since they were actually in the opposite corner from where the employee had pointed. A while later, we entered the Wal-Mart store and asked the same question. The response was considerably different. The associate cheerfully led us directly to the light bulb selection and asked if there was anything else she could help us find. This may seem like a trivial matter to some people, but you can't help coming away from a Wal-Mart store believing that you received a higher level of service than at a competitor's store.

Kmart

Kmart was a spin-off from the S. S. Kresge Company in 1962 as a discount general merchandise chain. The first store opened in Garden City, Michigan on March 1, 1962, just a few months before Sam Walton opened his first Wal-Mart store. In fact, Sam Walton reportedly inspected the new Kmart stores carefully as he was deciding to build his first Wal-Mart store. Harry Cunningham, a vice president for Kresge, became the chief executive officer of Kmart. In contrast to Wal-Mart, the Kmart chain grew very rapidly in the early years. By the end of 1963 there were 53 Kmart stores with sales of $83 million. At the end of 1973, the company was operating 673 stores generating $4.1 billion in sales. By 1974 the company had stores in all 48 contiguous states and Canada, thus becoming the first truly national discount store chain.

Strategies

Kmart's locational strategy was considerably different from that of Wal-Mart. Kmart spread rapidly across the country, locating in larger cities, in effect leaving the smaller communities for Wal-Mart and the regional discounters. In addition, Kmart opened stores in Canada and Australia in the 1960s.

Many of the early Kmart stores were relatively large for that era, ranging up to 115,000 square feet. In the early stores many of the departments were leased departments, operated by companies such as Dunham's Sporting Goods, Shoe Corporation of America, Helzberg's Diamond Shops, etc. As time went on, however, Kmart acquired many of these companies and integrated them into the stores as Kmart departments. Likewise, many of the early Kmart stores had an adjacent grocery store operated by Allied Supermarkets. Over a period of time, Kmart established relationships with other grocery lessees, and included supermarkets in new stores in a more random fashion. As Kmart started introducing smaller stores of approximately 40,000 square feet in smaller towns in the mid-1970s, supermarkets were usually not included.

Kmart's marketing strategy from the beginning was to enhance its discount image by having a sale a week. The circulars announcing these sale items were usually inserted in local print publications or in some cases mailed to households. In addition, Kmart became famous for its in-store blue light specials. Throughout the day, on a seemingly random basis, announcements are made over the public address system concerning an item that is being offered for a few minutes at a deep discount from the regular price. Attention is called to the sale by a rotating blue light and a public address announcement. The blue light specials are usually clearance items, but sometimes are extended to include other things such as bargain hotdogs from the snack bar.

By 1976, Kmart had over 1,000 stores with $8.4 billion in sales, and its growth seemed unstoppable. It had become the second largest retailer, in the United States, behind Sears Roebuck. At the end of 1980, Kmart had over 2,000 stores, but its sales still lagged behind those of Sears Roebuck. In the mid-1980s, the company started acquiring specialty store chains. For example, in 1984 it acquired Home Centers of America, later renamed Builders Square; and also Waldenbooks stores. In 1985, Kmart acquired Pay Less Drug Stores, an Oregon-based drug store chain.

In 1989, Kmart launched a membership warehouse club business, known as Pace. In the same year, Kmart purchased The Sports Authority and quickly expanded it well beyond its Florida origin. In 1991, Kmart acquired full ownership of OfficeMax. Borders book store was purchased in 1992 and combined with Walden Book Company to become Borders-Walden Group in 1993.

In 1993 Kmart sold most of its Pace membership clubs to Wal-Mart and closed the remaining clubs. Also in 1993, Kmart sold the Pay Less Drug Store chain.

Figure 2-3 shows Kmart sales from 1988 to 1993. Note that Kmart total sales has only grown by $8.3 billion since 1988, while Wal-Mart's sales during the same period grew by $46.7 billion.

Target

The Target chain of discount stores was spun off from the Dayton department store chain, headquartered in Minneapolis. The first Target store opened in May of 1962 in the St. Paul suburb of Roseville, just two months after Kmart opened its first store, and about three months before Sam Walton opened his first Wal-Mart store. Most of the early Target stores included an adjacent leased supermarket, in a manner similar to Kmart's early strategy. By 1968 the Target chain had grown to 11 stores and then grew to 67 stores by 1978, then to 341 stores by 1988 and by the end of 1993 had over 500 stores.

Figure 2-3 Kmart Net Sales

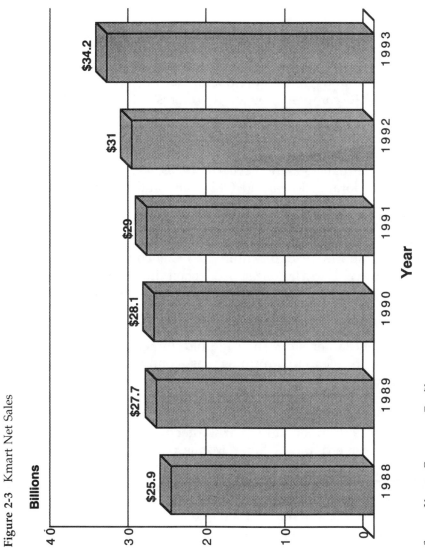

Source: Kmart Corporate Profile

Strategies

Target's locational strategy was less well-defined than those of Wal-Mart and Kmart. In general, the strategy focused on market dominance in certain key markets. The company sort of jumped around the country in its store openings. After the initial stores in Minnesota, the company opened two stores in Denver in 1966, two stores in St. Louis in 1968 and six stores in Texas and Oklahoma in 1969.

In the years ahead, Target also turned to acquisitions as a method of expansion. In the early 1970s, it acquired 16 Arlans stores in Colorado, Iowa and Oklahoma and converted them to Target stores. In 1980 Target acquired the 40 unit Ayr-Way chain along with its Indianapolis distribution center. In 1982, Target acquired 33 FedMarts, 28 of which were located in Southern California, and in 1986, it acquired 50 Gemco stores, all of which were converted to Target stores. Then in 1989, the company acquired 31 Gold Circle and Richway stores in Georgia, Florida and North Carolina.

In 1990, Target opened its first Target Greatland store, a considerably larger store than the old Targets. Merchandise was displayed in lifestyle groupings as contrasted to commodity groups in the past (similar to furniture stores that have room groupings rather than all the sofas together, etc.) In sticking with its market dominance strategy, the company opened 19 stores in one day in 1991. In the same year, Target opened 85,000 square foot stores in Brainerd and Willmar, Minnesota, signaling its intention to start competing in the smaller markets long dominated by Wal-Mart and, to some extent, by Kmart. In 1993, Target opened 12 stores in the Chicago area in one day.

Target stores have the image of being upscale discount department stores and the company strives to maintain this image. In my opinion, they may be slightly more upscale in apparel, featuring private label merchandise such as Merona and Honors. But there is little difference in the other merchandise handled. For example, just like Wal-Mart and Kmart, Target stocks Black & Decker power tools, Stanley hand tools, Fram oil filters, Glidden paint, Roadmaster bicycles, etc. The perception of higher quality merchandise comes from the layout of the store and the comparatively good lighting. Unlike Wal-Mart and Kmart, Target usually doesn't clutter its aisles with a lot of dump bins and gondolas. This gives a cleaner look to the store. However, like Wal-Mart, the apparel in Target stores is displayed over a carpeted area, giving it a classier look compared to being displayed over a tile floor. Target stores also have good lighting and a bright color scheme, giving the stores a fresher look than some of their competitors. Dayton Hudson, the parent company of Target, is known for its upscale traditional department stores and a few of the "tricks" learned in that trade may have been carried over to the Target stores in the form of displays and signage.

Target's sales are shown for every two years from 1983 to 1993 in Figure 2-4. Although sales more than doubled from 1987 to 1993, Wal-Mart's sales more than quadrupled during the same time period. Target's sales are still only about one-third those of Kmart. Target's parent company, Dayton-Hudson, has traditional department stores also and has not been as aggressive in expanding its discount stores.

MEMBERSHIP WAREHOUSE CLUBS

The first membership warehouse club, sometimes referred to as a *wholesale club* was opened by Sol Price in San Diego in 1976. The early clubs were aimed at providing small retailers with merchandise for resale and supplies needed in their own business. But as time went on, increasing numbers of consumers started shopping the clubs as they became aware of the savings in the low overhead operations.

By the 1980s, the membership warehouse concept was starting to catch on across the country, and sales increased dramatically through the early 1990s. Table 2-1 shows the growth in the number of stores and sales from 1983 through 1992. The most dramatic point of the table is that sales for membership warehouses grew from less than $1 billion in 1983 to nearly $35 billion in 1992.

Figure 2-5 shows the market share of each of the major warehouse clubs (Sam's, Price Club, Pace, B.J.'s, and Costco). Sam's bought most of the Pace clubs from Kmart, and Price Club

Figure 2-4 Target Net Sales

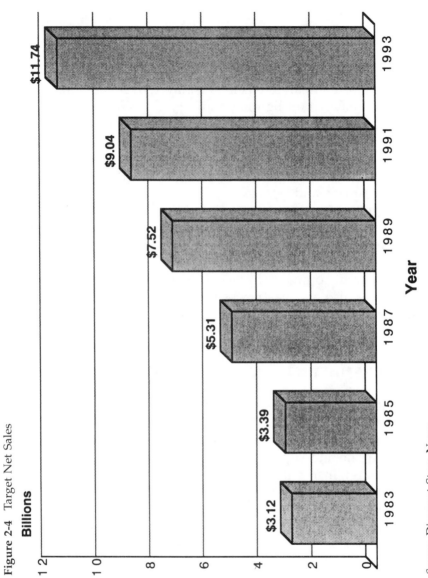

Billions

$11.74

$9.04

$7.52

$5.31

$3.39

$3.12

1 2

1 0

8

6

4

2

0

1983   1985   1987   1989   1991   1993

Year

Source: Discount Store News

Table 2-1 Ten Years of Wholesale Industry Growth, 1983-1992

Year	Stores	Sales ($Billions)
1983	21	0.9
1984	65	2.0
1985	118	4.2
1986	209	7.3
1987	257	10.7
1988	306	13.9
1989	367	17.5
1990	407	22.1
1991	495	27.8
1992	588	34.7

Source: Cornell University, 1992

and Costco merged. This left two major players in the membership warehouse business plus a few smaller contenders. Because of overbuilding in the 1980s and early 1990s, there are indications that the club business is saturated. In 1993 and 1994, same store sales for most of the clubs have been down. In other words, stores that had been open at least a year experienced lower sales than in the previous year.

Membership warehouse clubs are usually large stores, ranging from 80,000 square feet to 140,000 square feet in size. They are very austere operations typically with bare concrete floors, unfinished ceilings and warehouse shelving. Much of the merchandise is placed on the shelves in pallets, using a fork lift. Most of these stores have evolved to a point where about half their sales are groceries. A lot of merchandise is sold in large packs referred to as *club packs*. For example, one can buy 24 roll packs of toilet tissue, 12 roll packs of paper towels, etc. Much of the grocery items are sold in institutional size containers, such as three pound boxes of corn flakes, two gallon containers of mayonnaise, catsup, etc., and two gallon jugs of liquid detergent. Much of the canned goods are sold by the case only.

Warehouse clubs operate on a very thin gross profit margin, ranging from 8% to 12% of sales. Therefore it is necessary to keep operating costs very low. In addition to the austere facilities, operating costs are also cut by drop shipping much of the merch-

Figure 2-5 Wholesale Club Market Share, 1991

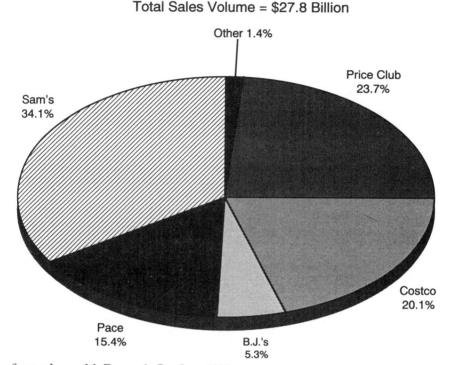

Total Sales Volume = $27.8 Billion

Other 1.4%

Price Club
23.7%

Sam's
34.1%

Costco
20.1%

Pace
15.4%

B.J.'s
5.3%

Source: James M. Degan & Co., Inc., 1992

andise directly from the factory to the store. These clubs usually stock only 5,000 to 15,000 sku's, so consequently they do not have a very good selection. They depend heavily on membership dues which usually run from $25 to $35 per person per year, with discounts for multiple membership within a business. Ostensibly, the clubs are set up to serve small retailers who might bring their cars or trucks to the club and haul back small amounts of merchandise for resale or for use in the business. However, all the clubs offer memberships to ordinary consumers who meet minimal requirements such as belonging to a credit union, working for a governmental agency, etc. And, in fact, a big share of the sales at the clubs are made to consumers rather than to businesses.

The clubs capture substantial business from grocery stores, office supply stores, and a few others. However, because of their limited selection, they do not have nearly as much impact on other local merchants as do discount general merchandise stores.

"CATEGORY KILLER" STORES

"Category killer" stores are relatively large stores that specialize in a fairly narrow line of merchandise. They are called category killer stores because they have a huge selection within a narrow category of merchandise and "kill" off the smaller stores in that category that have limited selections. In most cases, store personnel also know the merchandise. These types of stores typically require a high traffic count to be feasible. This means that they normally locate in mid- to large-sized cities. However, some of the chains are experimenting with smaller format stores that may be feasible in smaller cities. Some of the leading stores in a few of the categories will be discussed.

Building Supply

The retail building supply industry is undergoing rapid and radical change. In general, traditional hardware stores and lumber yards are rapidly disappearing, and customers are flocking to category killer businesses such as Home Depot, Builders Square, Home Quarters, Lowes, etc. Consumers like the large selections and the perceived lower prices. Home Depot is the largest of these chains, in terms of sales.

Home Depot

Home Depot offers a clear overview of its business: in its 1993 annual report "Founded in 1978 in Atlanta, Georgia, The Home Depot is the world's largest home improvement retailer and ranks among the 20 largest retailers in the United States. At the close of fiscal 1993, the company was operating 264 full-service warehouse-style stores in 23 states. The average Home Depot store is approximately 99,900 square feet, with an additional 20,000–29,000 square feet of outside selling and storage area. The stores stock approximately 30,000 different kinds of building materials, home improvement supplies, and lawn and garden products. The company employs approximately 57,000 people. The majority of the company's stores now offer installation of home improvement products, a service planned to be extended to all Home Depot stores within the next year." Figure 2-6 shows the rapid increase in Home Depot's sales in the last eight years, growing from $1.01 billion in fiscal 1986 to $9.24 billion in fiscal 1993. Figure 2-7 shows the number of Home Depot stores by state. Appendix 2 lists the cities and addresses of Home Depot stores.

In 1993, Home Depot's gross profit margin was 27.6% of sales, and its operating expenses were 20.0%. Its after-tax net income was 5.0% of sales. On the other hand, Wal-Mart's 1993 gross profit margin was 20.6%, its operating costs were 15.3% and its net profit after taxes was 3.5% of sales. The Wal-Mart figures are consolidated for all company businesses and are biased downward slightly because of the austere operations of the Sam's Clubs.

It is interesting to compare the differences between the two companies. One would have to conclude that overall, prices on comparable items probably sell for more at Home Depot. The primary reason is that Home Depot has to mark up prices from the supplier more so that it can cover its higher operating costs. Why are the operating costs higher? Without detailed data, my conclusion is that Home Depot is offering a higher level of service which means more and better trained associates, which is the main reason operating costs are higher.

Consumer Electronics

The category killer consumer electronics stores handle audio and video equipment. They also sell computers and software. Many sell major appliances such as washers, driers, dishwashers, stoves and microwave ovens. Their sales are increasing at a rapid rate. The top five chains at the end of 1992 are listed in Table 2-2.

Figure 2-6 Home Depot Net Sales

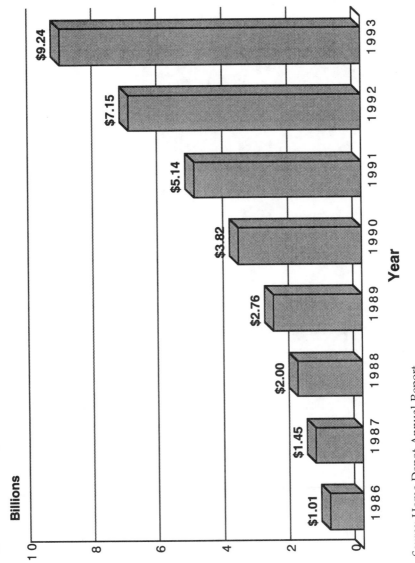

Billions

10

8

6

4

2

0

$1.01 1986
$1.45 1987
$2.00 1988
$2.76 1989
$3.82 1990
$5.14 1991
$7.15 1992
$9.24 1993

Year

Source: Home Depot Annual Report

Figure 2-7 Number of Home Depot Stores by State

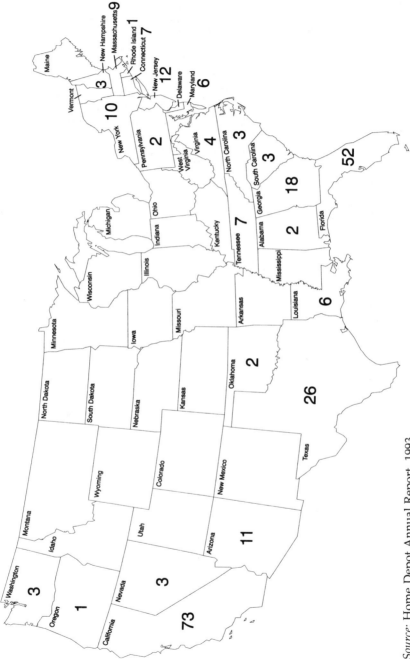

Source: Home Depot Annual Report, 1993

Table 2-2. Top 5 Consumer Electronics Stores

Chain	1992 Sales	Number of Stores
Circuit City	$3.27 billion	260
Best Buy	$1.62 billion	111
Silo	$970 million	204
The Good Guys	$504 million	41
Fretters	$362 million	86

Office Supplies

The stores in this category are relatively large (15,000 to 30,000 square feet) and they handle office equipment, office furniture and all types of office supplies. The four largest chains are shown in Table 2-3.

Sporting Goods

The category killer sporting goods stores range in size from 10,000 to 40,000 square feet. Most of them have several departments handling a good assortment of merchandise. The top five chains are shown in Table 2-4.

There are other category-dominant stores, but many are so new that they are in a state of flux, with mergers and acquisitions occurring at a rapid rate.

Factory Outlet Malls

Factory outlet malls originated on the East Coast, but have migrated across the United States. In the earlier years, many were located downtown in vacated factories or warehouses. Now, most of the malls are located on an interstate highway, and within commuting distance of population centers.

A few developers seem to be developing chains such as Tanger Outlet Malls or VF Factory Outlet Malls. They vary in size according to the market, from 8 or 10 stores up to 75 to 100 stores.

Table 2-3. Top 4 Office Supply Stores

Chain	1992 Sales	Number of Stores
Office Depot	$1.73 billion	284
Staples	$883 million	174
BizMart	$650 million	105
Office Max	$528 million	179

Table 2-4. Top 5 Sporting Goods Stores

Chain	1992 Sales	Number of Stores
Herman's	$580 million	253
Sports Authority	$412 million	56
Oshman's	$313 million	183
Big 5 Sporting Goods	$270 million	150
Sportsmart	$251 million	31

The preponderance of the stores are apparel stores, but more and more housewares stores, book stores, and other specialty stores are appearing in the new malls.

There are no good studies showing the sales of factory outlet malls, overall. However, where they have located in states with good sales tax data (such as Iowa), it is obvious that they generate considerable sales, with $20 million to $60 million per year being fairly common.

Specialty Mail Order

Mail order houses have changed over the last several decades. The early mail order catalogs such as Sears Roebuck, Montgomery Ward and JCPenney's were general catalogs that tried to provide all things to all people. In the last several years, however, the general mail order houses have disappeared and there has been a great proliferation of specialty mail order houses.

There are so many catalogs today that there are "catalogs of catalogs." Most of these catalogs have become very specialized. For example there are catalogs of computer supplies, office supplies, sick room supplies, camping supplies, and so on.

There are no comprehensive studies of the market share or impact of mail order houses on other businesses. However, anecdotally, it seems that many people do order something from mail order houses at one time or another.

Improved telecommunications services and overnight delivery services have contributed to the apparent resurgence of mail order houses. We can call in orders on toll-free telephone lines, or we can fax or E-mail them in a few seconds. If needed, we can get delivery the next day.

It appears that interactive electronic mail order will be a reality within a few years. By using a computer or an interactive cable TV system, consumers will be able to call up the type of merchandise they are interested in and see comparisons of benefits, features and prices.

These new specialized mail order systems will not be for everyone but they will appeal to busy people who feel comfortable using modern technology.

SUMMARY

It is apparent that the number of discount mass merchandisers has increased dramatically in the last decade or two. Many customers have been attracted to them because of their perceived lower prices and their large selections. In addition, they usually provide plenty of free parking and convenient shopping hours, including 24 hours a day and seven days a week for some stores.

The major formats are listed below.

• Discount General Merchandise Stores. Included are stores such as: Wal-Mart, Kmart, Target and several other regional chains and range in size from 40,000 square feet to 130,000 square feet. Most will have between 30 and 40 departments, handling up to 80,000 stock keeping units (sku's).

• Membership Warehouse Clubs. 1993 was a year of consolidations for the clubs. Wal-Mart bought the Pace clubs from Kmart and converted them to Sam's clubs. The Price Club merged with

Costco to form Price/Costco. The only other chain of any size is B.J.'s, located in the Eastern United States.

These stores tend to be between 100,000 square feet and 150,000 square feet in size and have evolved to where half their sales is in bulk food. Most of these stores only handle between 5,000 and 15,000 stock keeping units (sku's), a rather limited selection.

The stores operate on a very thin gross profit margin and depend heavily on membership fees which average around $25 per member per year. The same store sales of these companies has been declining in the last year, leading many experts to conclude that the market is nearly saturated with clubs.

• Category Killer Stores. These are large specialty stores that have a large selection that is attractively priced and is sold by employees who know the merchandise. This format is feasible primarily in larger market areas. Therefore, these stores are capturing substantial sales from local merchants in the cities and from surrounding smaller towns.

Home Depot, in the home improvement area, is the largest of these chains, but other chains are appearing in many categories such as toys, office supplies, books, pet supplies and several others.

• Factory Outlet Malls. These are stores grouped in a mall setting usually along an interstate highway, within commuting distance of population centers. Manufacturers market various merchandise through these outlets, including firsts, seconds, overruns, reconditioned merchandise, etc.

Many of these stores claim to sell merchandise at half-price or lower and attract, not only travellers from the highways, but destination shoppers within a two hour commute. They particularly impact local merchants who sell the same brand of merchandise.

• Mail Order Houses. Mail order has evolved from general catalogs to specialty catalogs. There are thousands of specialty mail order houses today. Many can sell at low prices because of low operating costs. Furthermore with the improvements in telecommunications and delivery service, the catalog houses can get merchandise to customers in a hurry. Specialty mail order seems to appeal to busy people, hobbyists and people located in remote areas.

The various formats discussed above have greatly increased in number and sales in the last decade. Together they are taking a larger share of the consumer's dollar. Nevertheless, there are still many opportunities for local merchants and small chain stores to fill niches and meet special needs.

3

IMPACTS OF THE DISCOUNT MASS MERCHANDISERS

Discount mass merchandise stores have an impact on local trade areas because they usually sell merchandise for a lower price and because they are usually relatively large stores. There is a principle in economics called "zero sum game" that applies to a trade area. It simply means that for a game in which the pot or "stakes" is fixed in size, when one player wins, the other players will lose an amount equal to the first player's winnings. This same principle applies to a large number of trade areas in the United States. If the population and income are relatively fixed in a market area, then the opening of a large new discount mass merchandise store will take a sizable slice out of a "fixed size retail pie," and some other merchants in the trade area will suffer equivalent losses of sales. In other words, some will have to settle for "smaller slices" of the retail "pie".

It is important to note that the loss of sales impacts not only retailers in the same community, but also more severely reduces the sales of businesses in outlying smaller communities that do *not* have a critical mass of retailing needed to keep customers shopping closer to home. It is also important to note that in parts of the country where the population and income are growing, local trade areas can accommodate the introduction of more new stores without necessarily reducing the sales of existing businesses because, in these situations, there is a growing retail pie.

What effect do the new discount stores have on other businesses? The truth is there have not been a lot of studies done on the subject as of this time. Those that have been done have usually been constrained to a specific type of discount store in a limited geographical area. However, most of the studies that have been done have come up with similar findings, and they verify what most of us intuitively know. I use two rules of thumb to describe the general impacts.

Rule of thumb number one is that merchants selling items that differ from those sold by the discount mass merchandisers will probably not experience a loss of sales. In fact, if these stores are near the discount stores, they often experience an increase in sales after the discount store opens because they benefit from the "spillover" of the additional traffic generated by the discounter.

Rule of thumb number two is that merchants selling the same things that the discount stores are selling will probably experience a decrease in sales after the discounter opens. This applies not only to merchants in the local area, but to those in the outlying areas. In some cases where merchants are able to re-position their stores to avoid competing head on with the discounters, they can often hold their own and sometimes actually gain sales. However, this would probably apply to a minority of the merchants.

THE IOWA STUDY: ANALYZING DISCOUNT GENERAL MERCHANDISE STORES

My study of the impact of Wal-Mart stores in Iowa was one of the first studies of its kind in the country. The first version was completed in 1988. It has been updated each year since then to track the dynamics of the situation as more and more stores are added. The results discussed below include data for fiscal year 1993, the latest available.

The Iowa study uses sales tax data to determine changes in sales for various types of stores after Wal-Mart stores opened in the area. The stores are classified for two digit Standard Industrial Classification (SIC) codes as determined by the federal government. In other words, the stores are classified in broad categories such as general merchandise, home furnishings, eating & drinking, apparel, etc.

Pull Factor Analysis

The data from the sales tax reports are in current dollars (not adjusted for price inflation). Current dollar figures are not a very satisfactory way of analyzing retail trends. They do not account for price inflation, population changes, or changes in a state's economy. The current dollar sales were converted to pull factors in this study to provide a more equitable basis for comparison. I developed the *pull factor concept* along with former graduate student, James McConnon, Jr. in 1980. The pull factor is merely the sales per person (per capita sales) in a town divided by the per capita sales for the state.

For example, if a town had per capita sales of $8,000 per year and the statewide per capita sales were $8,000 per year, the pull factor would be $8,000 divided by $8,000 to equal 1.0. The interpretation would be that the town was selling to the equivalent of 100% of the town population, in full-time customer equivalents. In other words, the pull factor is a proxy measure for the size of the retail trade area of the town. The larger the pull factor, the larger the trade area. When data are available, pull factors can be computed for the different merchandise categories within a town and for the total sales of the town.

Comparison Techniques

Pull factors were computed for eight merchandise categories for towns over 5,000 population from the establishment of the first

Wal-Mart stores (1983) to 1993. These were compared to the average pull factors for the non-Wal-Mart towns (between 5,000 and 30,000 population). Comparisons were also made to larger cities and smaller towns.

Some of the non-Wal-Mart towns had Kmart or Target stores and usually one or more regional discount stores. On average, the non-Wal-Mart towns suffered losses in sales in most categories—except food—over the years that Wal-Mart stores were being built in the state. It appears that over the years, more and more shoppers left these towns to shop in the Wal-Mart towns or in the cities.

Throughout the remainder of this discussion, towns that have Wal-Mart stores will be referred to as *Wal-Mart towns* and towns in the control group that did not have Wal-Mart stores will be referred to as *non-Wal-Mart towns*.

The net result of the study is a broad look at the change in trade area sizes for stores in different merchandise categories in the host towns and in other competing towns. It cannot be stated conclusively that Wal-Mart stores caused all the changes in trade area size, since other variables are always interacting to cause changes. However, when significant changes are seen to be consistently correlated with the opening of Wal-Mart stores, one can draw solid conclusions in spite of the lack of more sophisticated statistical techniques.

Pull Factor Comparison for Wal-Mart Towns vs. Non-Wal-Mart Towns

It was stated earlier that the pull factor is a proxy measure for the size of the trade area of a town. The following discussion will refer to various charts to compare the change in trade area size for different types of stores in Wal-Mart towns and non-Wal-Mart towns.

Most of the Wal-Mart towns experienced an immediate increase in trade area size in the first year that the Wal-Mart store opened. There were a few exceptions to this, usually involving a nearby city opening a new mall or a group of large stores at about the same time the smaller town was opening its Wal-Mart store.

The 1993 study included 34 towns with population below 30,000 that had Wal-Mart stores. There were 17 same size towns that did not have a Wal-Mart store. The changes in sales (pull factors) for both the Wal-Mart towns and the non-Wal-Mart towns are discussed in the following sections.

General Merchandise Stores

General merchandise stores are department stores and variety stores including Wal-Mart, Kmart, Target, Sears, Penneys, variety stores and others. Since Wal-Mart stores are in this category, one would expect to see sales increase. Conversely, the non-Wal-Mart towns would be expected to show a steady decline in the pull factor.

Figure 3-1 shows that the towns that Wal-Mart entered had slightly weaker general merchandise stores, selling to an average of 140% of the town population, while the general merchandise stores in non Wal-Mart towns were selling to the equivalent of 155% of the town population. However, in the first year after a Wal-Mart opening, its host town's pull factor jumped to 2.15 indicating that it was now selling to 215% of the town population. That number decreased to 201% after five years, but that was still 43.6% over the base year as indicated in Figure 3-1. Obviously, most of the gain was experienced by the Wal-Mart stores, and usually at the expense of competing general merchandise stores.

The decline in sales after the first year in the Wal-Mart towns was probably due to two factors; 1) the closing of competing general merchandise stores, and 2) the addition of nearby new Wal-Mart stores that capture some trade from existing Wal-Mart stores. Existing general merchandise stores were usually hit hard after Wal-Mart stores opened. It was common for some of the regional discount general merchandisers to close their stores within a year or two after Wal-Mart opened. At the same time, the Wal-Mart Company has a saturation strategy, whereby they con-

Figure 3-1 Changes in General Merchandise Store Sales

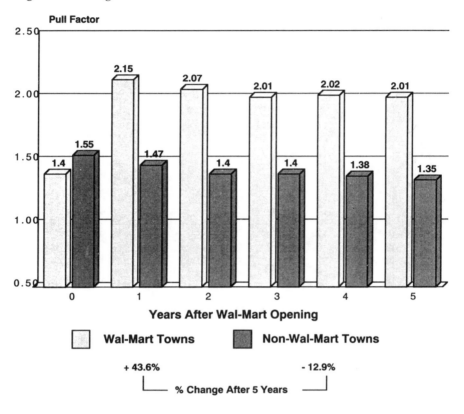

Source. Kenneth E. Stone study.

tinue to fill in the gaps between existing stores with new stores, until the Wal-Mart stores are competing with each other. (This was stated by Sam Walton in his autobiography, *Sam Walton, Made in America.*)

Sales of department stores and variety stores in the non-Wal-Mart towns continually decreased over the years. Figure 3-1 shows the decline worsening by 12.9% after five years. This is in stark contrast to the gains of over 40% in the Wal-Mart towns. It appears that most of this trade was captured by the Wal-Mart towns, since the larger cities actually lost general merchandise sales during this period.

Figure 3-2 Changes in Home Furnishing Store Sales

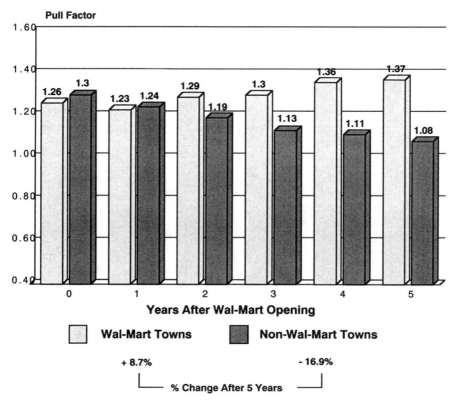

Source. Kenneth E. Stone study

Home Furnishings Stores

Home furnishings stores consist of furniture stores, major appliance stores, floor covering stores and consumer electronic stores. Figure 3-2 shows that the towns that Wal-Mart entered had slightly weaker home furnishing stores than the non-Wal-Mart towns. During the first five years, the Wal-Mart towns' pull factor went from 1.26 to 1.37, while the non-Wal-Mart town declined from 1.30 to 1.08.

These types of stores quite often experienced an increase in sales in the Wal-Mart town because much of what they sold was unique and not sold at a Wal-Mart store. Therefore, these stores tended to benefit from the spillover of traffic that came ostensibly to shop at the Wal-Mart store.

Figure 3-2 shows a slight downturn in home furnishings sales in the Wal-Mart towns the first year, but then a progressive increase in sales, with sales being up an average of 8.7% after five years. In one Iowa town of 15,000 population, a very good furniture store had been located on the edge of town for many years. Then about four years ago, Wal-Mart opened a new store across the street within a few hundred yards. It cannot be proven that the traffic generated by the Wal-Mart store helped the furniture store, but this year the owner of the furniture store completed a large addition to the building and had a new grand opening to celebrate.

Much like general merchandise, the home furnishings stores in non-Wal-Mart towns continually lost sales over the first five years that Wal-Mart stores were operational. Figure 3-2 indicates that sales declined by 16.9% after five years. Again, this is quite a contrast to the Wal-Mart towns that increased sales in this category by nearly 9% after five years. Since home furnishings tend to be big ticket items that are purchased infrequently, many shoppers are willing to travel further to check prices and selection. Apparently some shoppers chose to purchase these items in the Wal-Mart towns, while some chose to purchase them in the bigger cities.

Eating and Drinking Places

Eating and drinking places usually benefit from the traffic generated by a nearby Wal-Mart store. More and more people are eating out all the time, and since Wal-Mart stores draw people from a large trade area, many choose to eat in restaurants in the Wal-Mart towns.

The trade area size for eating and drinking places in both Wal-Mart towns and non-Wal-Mart towns was identical, with each selling 126% of the town population before Wal-Mart stores entered the scene. However, after five years, the Wal-Mart towns'

Figure 3-3 Changes in Eating and Drinking Store Sales

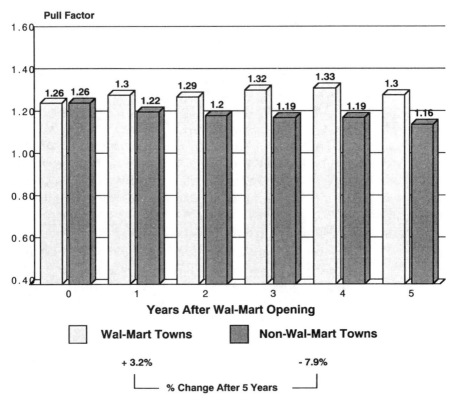

Source. Kenneth E. Stone study.

pull factor had grown to 130%, while the non-Wal-Mart towns had declined to 116% as shown in Figure 3-3.

Figure 3-3 shows that sales for eating and drinking establishments in Wal-Mart towns were 3.2% higher than the state average five years after the store opened. Even though Wal-Mart stores have a snack bar, it does not offer much competition for the local restaurants.

Even though more and more people are eating out all the time, they apparently choose to coordinate some of their dining out with their shopping trips. Consequently, the non-Wal-Mart towns are losing restaurant sales to the Wal-Mart towns. Figure 3-3 shows eating and drinking sales declining by 7.9% after five years.

Apparel Stores

Apparel stores consist of men's, women's and children's clothing stores along with shoe stores. The comparison of trade areas for apparel is interesting. The towns in which Wal-Mart stores opened had relatively weaker apparel stores, selling only to the equivalent of 140% of the population, while the non-Wal-Mart towns had larger trade areas, selling to the equivalent of 160% of the towns' population. Although sales for all towns deteriorated, the non-Wal-Mart towns pull factor five years later is about where the Wal-Mart towns started before Wal-Mart opened their stores. As Figure 3-4 shows, the apparel trade area for non-Wal-Mart towns is substantially larger than for the Wal-Mart towns five years after the introduction of Wal-Mart stores.

In the Wal-Mart towns, overall sales of apparel stores continued to decrease from over 7% the first year to nearly 18% five years later, as shown in Figure 3-4. Many of the local apparel stores in the towns where Wal-Mart opened stores were positioned at the low end of the price range, thereby putting the local merchant in direct competition with the new discount store, and these are the stores that suffered reductions in sales. Some towns that had a preponderance of more upscale clothing stores actually saw the sales of their local stores increase after Wal-Mart opened. Men's clothing stores also contributed to the decline in local apparel store sales since they have experienced declines due to the "dressing down of men," as will be discussed later.

In the non-Wal-Mart towns, sales in apparel stores declined, but fared slightly better than sales in the Wal-Mart towns. Figure 3-4 shows the decrease in sales ranging from 7.5% the first year to 13.1% after five years.

Specialty Stores

According to the SIC code, specialty stores consist of the following.

- Drug stores
- Card and gift shops

Figure 3-4 Changes in Apparel Store Sales

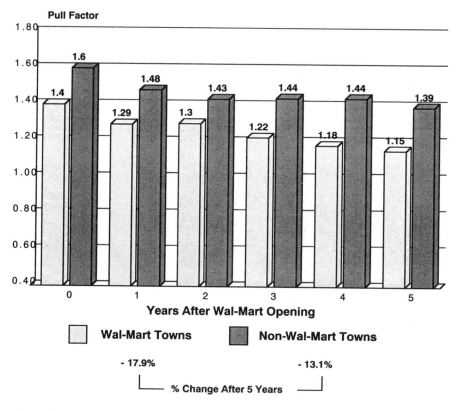

Source. Kenneth E. Stone study.

- Sporting goods stores
- Jewelry stores
- Book stores
- Hobby, toy and game stores
- Camera and photo supply stores
- Luggage and leather goods stores
- Other miscellaneous stores such as fabric stores

The trade area sizes for Wal-Mart towns and non-Wal-Mart towns were very close before Wal-Mart stores opened. Figure 3-5 shows that sales in all these stores declined over the five year period; however, they declined by a greater amount in the non-

Figure 3-5 Changes in Specialty Store Sales

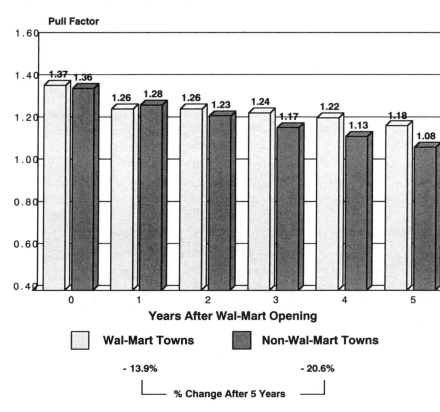

Source. Kenneth E. Stone study.

Wal-Mart towns. Apparently some of these stores were losing sales to the Wal-Mart stores and some to specialty stores in the bigger cities.

In the Wal-Mart towns most specialty stores were competing, at least partially, with one or more departments in a Wal-Mart store. Consequently, the specialty category suffered reductions in sales, ranging from 8% the first year to nearly 14% after five years, as shown in Figure 3-5. The primary towns not experiencing a reduction in specialty store sales were those involved in tourism. Apparently tourists patronized local specialty stores that sell unique merchandise. However, in most communities, when a discount mass merchandiser opens a store, it naturally follows that sales in specialty stores will decrease because many customers merely transfer their purchases from the specialty store to the discount store.

In the non-Wal-Mart towns, specialty store sales fared worse than they did in the Wal-Mart town. Figure 3-5 shows a decrease of 5.9% after one year, but a steady decline to 20.6% after five years. It appears that some of these purchases are being transferred to the Wal-Mart stores and some to the specialty stores in the bigger cities.

Building Materials Stores

Building materials stores consist of lumber yards, home repair stores, hardware stores, and paint, glass and wallpaper stores. Wal-Mart towns initially had slightly larger trade areas for building materials stores than did non-Wal-Mart towns, as shown in Figure 3-6. The sales declined somewhat proportionately until year five when the Wal-Mart towns experienced a substantial rebound. The introduction of "category killer" type stores in a couple of these towns is the likely explanation.

In the Wal-Mart towns, *hardware stores* seemed to take the brunt of the reduction in sales, because most of them have many departments that are directly competing with a department in a Wal-Mart store. Figure 3-6 shows the reduction in sales for these businesses after the first five years was 12.7%. However, some hardware store owners who were willing to reposition their stores so that they competed less directly with the discount store have fared remarkably well.

In the non- Wal-Mart towns, the erosion of building material sales seems to be steady and sharp. Figure 3-6 shows a first year decline of 6.9%, quickly degenerating to a 20.8% decline after five years. Apparently shoppers are buying some of this merchandise in the Wal-Mart stores. However, the majority of the purchases appear to be made in the bigger cities in the "category killer" stores.

Figure 3-6 Changes in Building Material Store Sales

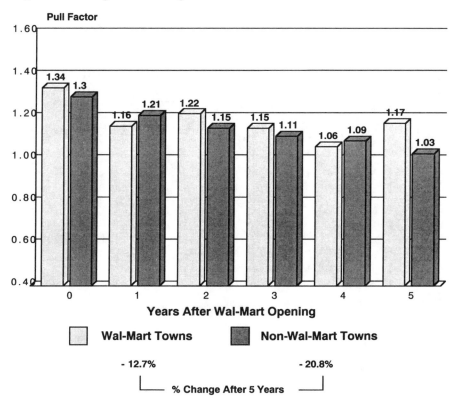

Source. Kenneth E. Stone study.

Food (Grocery Stores)

Most people, even grocers, do not realize that many items sold in a traditional supermarket are also sold in a discount general merchandise store. Therefore, they find it hard to believe that a town's grocery store sales decline slightly after a Wal-Mart store opens its doors. But 20 to 30% of the merchandise sold in the traditional supermarket is also sold in a discount general merchandise store. In addition to a small assortment of non-perishable foods, discount general merchandise stores usually carry health and beauty aids, cleaning supplies, paper products, pet supplies,

Figure 3-7 Changes in Grocery Store Sales

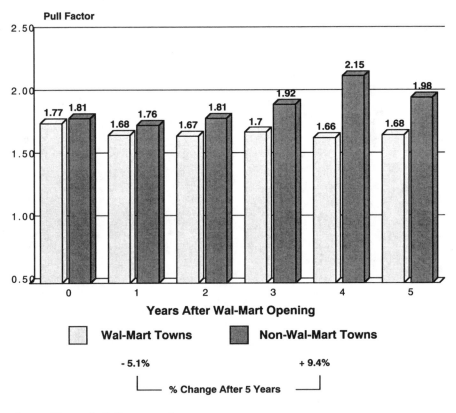

Source. Kenneth E. Stone study.

greeting cards and books and magazines, all of which are sold in a typical supermarket. The problem is that many consumers *believe* that these items are lower priced in the discount store, so they buy the food in the supermarket and make a special trip to the discount store to purchase the non- food items. Simply visit several discount general merchandise stores and observe what shoppers are putting in their shopping carts. Most people are amazed to find customers buying considerable amounts of merchandise that was once purchased at the supermarket. Careful price checks, however, reveal that the supermarkets actually may be lower priced on some of these items.

Figure 3-7 shows that Wal-Mart towns initially had slightly smaller trade areas than the non-Wal-Mart towns (selling to 177% of the town population) but declined to 168% five years later. Conversely the non-Wal-Mart towns were selling to an average of 181% of the town population initially and increased to 198% in five years.

Figure 3-7 shows that the reduction in food store sales averaged 5.1% after the first five years. This is especially puzzling since Iowa has lost 845 grocery stores (43%) in the last 15 years. The stores are disappearing primarily from the smaller towns in the state (usually below 1,000 population). When a small town loses its last grocery store, the residents of that town have no choice but to go to a nearby larger town or city to shop for groceries. Therefore, these Wal-Mart towns should have gained grocery store sales, but they did not. On the other hand, as we have already seen, the non-Wal-Mart towns did experience an increase in grocery store sales.

The one bright spot in the non-Wal-Mart towns is food stores. Figure 3-7 shows that after a slight decline the first year, sales then continued to improve to a 9.4% increase after five years. The large increase in the fourth year appears to be an anomaly, whereby a few towns got new food stores that year, but had some drop out the next year. Apparently many people in the trade area make the non-Wal-Mart town a destination to shop for groceries, but do not spill over in an equivalent manner to shop for other merchandise.

Total Sales

Total sales for a community consists of the categories above plus a few other categories that are hard to analyze, such as services, utilities and miscellaneous. Figure 3-8 indicates that the Wal-Mart towns had overall smaller trade areas initially (126%) than the non-Wal-Mart towns (134%). However, after five years the Wal-Mart towns sold to 133% of the town population, whereas sales in

Figure 3-8 Changes in Total Sales

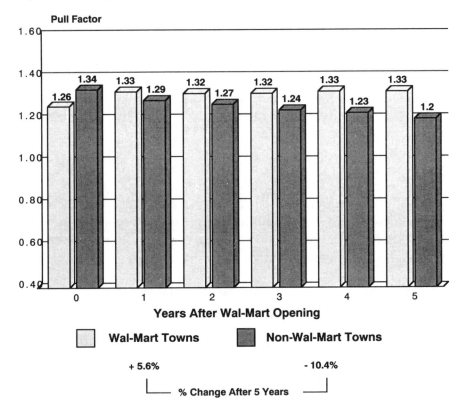

Source. Kenneth E. Stone study.

the non-Wal-Mart towns had declined to 120% of the town population.

Figure 3-8 shows that in the Wal-Mart towns total sales increased, 5.6% more than average for the state after the first five years. Although this is not a spectacular growth rate, it is certainly better than the decline in sales experienced by the towns that did not have a Wal-Mart store.

Total sales in the non-Wal-Mart towns continued to decline over the years. Figure 3-8 illustrates that sales declined by 3.7% the first year, but continued to decline to 10.4% by the end of five years. The primary conclusion is that as more and more Wal-Mart stores are built, they capture more and more of the trade from the non-Wal-Mart towns.

Other Winners in the Wal-Mart Towns

Although it could not be documented in individual towns, it is fairly clear that several other types of businesses are helped by the additional traffic that Wal-Mart stores bring into a community. Based on observations and anecdotal evidence, some of these types of stores are listed below.

- Upscale clothing stores
- Upscale shoe stores
- Upscale gift shops
- Upscale jewelry stores
- Gasoline stations
- Personal service facilities
- Business service facilities
- Any other unique store selling something different than the discount store

Effect of Store Saturation

Growth in total sales was an *average* for all towns. Unfortunately, not all towns had a sustained increase in sales. Some were the victims of Wal-Mart's own saturation strategy, where they placed other stores in nearby towns. Others had the misfortune of having nearby towns build new shopping malls. Eight towns had lower sales (pull factors) in 1993 than they had the year before Wal-Mart opened. Three other towns had pull factors that had grown by less than 2% by 1993. Figure 3-9 shows bar charts for Independence, Iowa, where the pull factor for total sales decreased from 1.27 the year before Wal-Mart opened to 1.22 in 1993, a decline of nearly 4%. All merchandise categories except general merchandise and eating and drinking showed a lower level of sales

Figure 3-9 Changes in Sales for Independence, Iowa

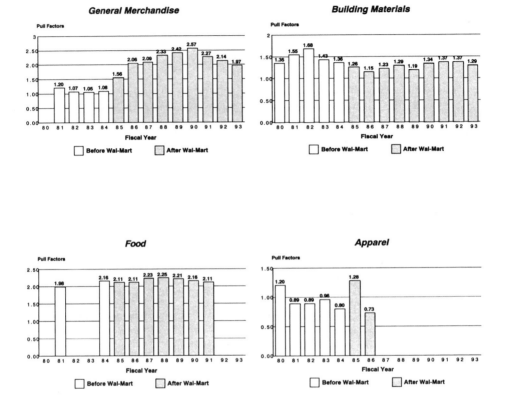

Source. Kenneth E. Stone study.

also. At least two Wal-Mart stores were built within 25 miles of Independence in recent years, probably explaining its decline in sales.

Fairfield, Iowa, a bigger town, experienced a reduction in its total sales pull factor from 1.33 in 1986 to 1.17 in 1993, a decline of 12%. All categories except general merchandise and home furnishings also showed a reduction in sales, as shown in Figure 3-10. A good sized shopping mall (including a Wal-Mart store) was built about 25 miles away in Ottumwa in 1989 and was probably the main cause of the loss of sales from Fairfield.

Figure 3-9 *(continued)*

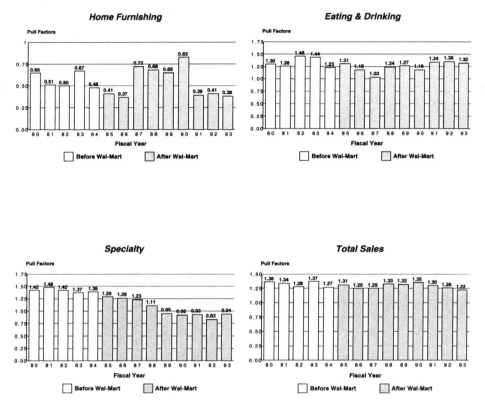

Source. Kenneth E. Stone study.

Effect on Outlying Smaller Towns

Smaller towns between 500 and 5,000 population within a 20-mile radius of each Wal-Mart town were compared to all other similar size towns further away from Wal-Mart towns. Figure 3-11 shows the results over five years. It is fairly obvious that nearby small towns lose trade more rapidly than others. After five years, the towns within a 20-mile radius of a Wal-Mart store had cumulative net sales reductions of 25.4%, while the non-Wal-Mart towns much further away had sales reductions of only 17.6%.

Figure 3-10 Changes in Sales for Fairfield, Iowa

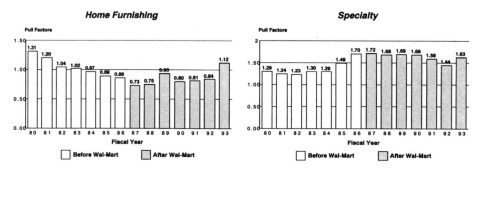

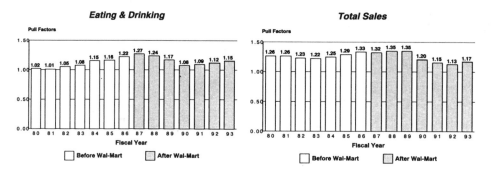

Source. Kenneth E. Stone study.

Overall Changes in Statewide Shopping Habits

The State of Iowa lists statewide sales for stores by three-digit SIC code. In other words, the change in statewide sales is listed in more detail than the sales by town that are listed by two digit SIC code. Therefore, it was possible to determine the change in per capita expenditures in different types of stores in more detail than has been discussed heretofore. Figure 3-12 shows the change in market share or per capita sales from 1983 (the first years that Wal-Mart stores opened in the state) to 1993 for a selected number of stores. Figure 3-13 shows the change in total dollars spent in various types of stores in the state in 1993 as compared to 1983.

Figure 3-10 *(continued)*

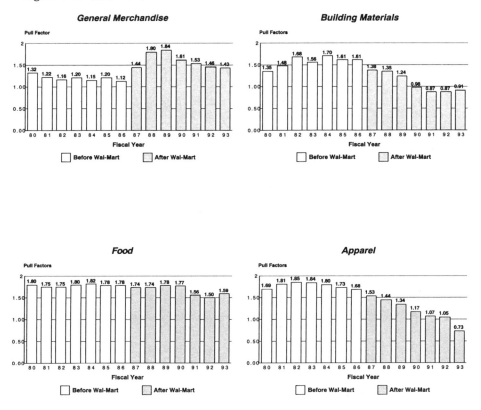

Source. Kenneth E. Stone study.

Department Stores

It can be seen that the average Iowan spent 31.7% more in department stores in 1993 than he or she did in 1983. Considering that discount department stores were nearly the only stores being built during this time, it is reasonable to assume that most of this increase was spent in these stores. Figure 3-13 shows that overall in 1993, $425.5 million more dollars were spent in department stores than in 1983.

Going to the other end of the chart 3-12, it can be seen that severe losses were experienced by several types of stores. A brief discussion of these stores follows.

Figure 3-11 Sales of Iowa Towns Within 20 Miles of Wal-Mart *vs.* Others of Same Size*

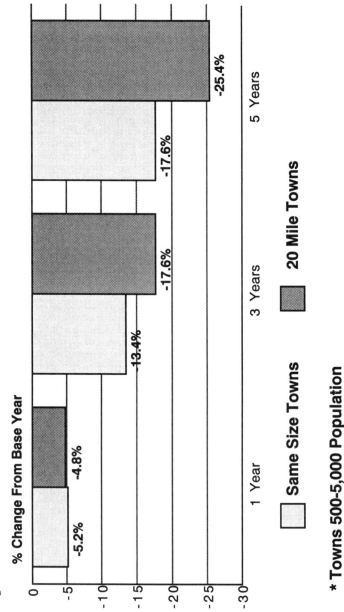

% Change From Base Year

-5.2%

-4.8%

-13.4%

-17.6%

-17.6%

-25.4%

1 Year

3 Years

5 Years

☐ Same Size Towns   ■ 20 Mile Towns

* Towns 500-5,000 Population

Figure 3-12 % Change in Market Share in Iowa Stores from 1983-1993

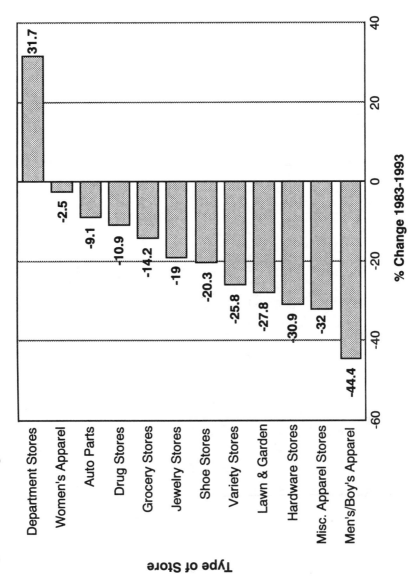

Figure 3-13 Dollar Change in Market Share in Iowa Stores From 1983-1993

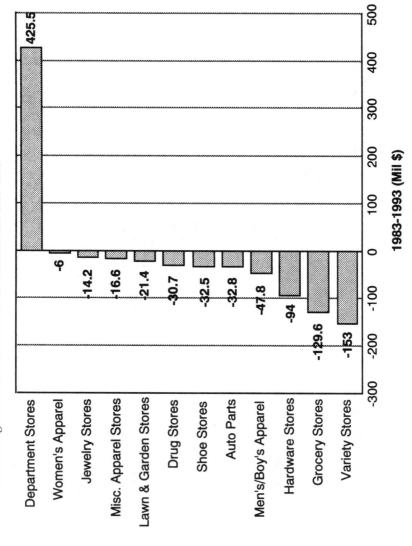

Men's and Boy's Apparel Stores

On average, Iowans spent 44.4% less in men's and boy's apparel stores in 1993 than in 1983. During that same time period, 50% of these types of stores went out of business. Stores such as Wal-Mart are not the sole reason for this trend. A significant percentage of men's and boy's apparel store losses attributable to the "dressing down" of men in America over the last ten years. Many large offices no longer require men to come to work in a coat and tie. Slacks and a sport shirt are acceptable now. Many corporations even have a weekly "casual day," where workers are encouraged to come to work in less formal clothes, such as jeans and a sweat shirt. Twenty years ago, many restaurants required a coat and tie for admittance. There are very few that require such formality today. In summary, men are not buying nearly as many dress clothes, but instead are buying casual attire, much of which can be purchased in department stores, including discount stores. Figure 3-13 indicates that the state of Iowa as a whole spent $47.5 million less in men's and boy's apparel stores in 1993 than in 1983.

Miscellaneous Apparel Stores

Per capita expenditures in miscellaneous apparel stores was 32% less in 1993 than it was in 1983. This would include maternity stores, large size shops, western wear, etc. Again, it appears that much of this merchandise is now being purchased in department stores. In terms of total dollars, state residents spent $16.6 million less in these stores in 1993 than in 1983.

Hardware Stores

The average Iowan spent almost 31% less in hardware stores in 1993 than in 1983. That translated to the loss of 37% of the hardware stores during that time. Stores like Wal-Mart and Kmart probably accounted for some of this loss, but the larger "category killer" stores such as Menard's and Pay Less Cashways were the real villain here, and in other states it would be stores such as Home Depot, Builder's Square and Lowes. Figure 3-13 shows that state residents spent $94 million less in hardware stores in 1993 than in 1983.

Lawn and Garden Centers

On average, Iowan's spent 27.8% less per person in lawn and garden centers in 1993 than in 1983. One only has to look at the sales generated by the mass merchandisers to see why. For the last several years Kmart has had the highest sales in lawn and garden of any company in the United States, followed closely by Wal-Mart. Companies such as Home Depot are also growing rapidly in this area. In terms of total dollars, the state spent $21.4 million less in 1993 in lawn and garden stores than in 1983.

Variety Stores

These stores, at one time called "five and dime stores," suffered substantial losses after the Wal-Mart stores came into the state. Iowans spent 25.8% less in them in 1993 than in 1983. Nearly everything sold in these stores was competing against the same merchandise in a Wal-Mart store. Many variety stores were locally owned and did not have the buying power of the national discount stores. Some of these stores tried to re-position their stores as primarily craft stores but, in the last few years, Wal-Mart has increased its selection of craft supplies, thereby countering the efforts of the variety stores.

Shoe Stores

Iowans spent 20.3% less in shoe stores in 1993 than in 1983. A lot of the low end shoes were purchased at the discount stores, rather than at the specialty stores. In addition, huge numbers of Americans have switched from dress shoes to athletic type sneakers, and many of these are purchased in sporting goods and department stores.

Jewelry Stores

The real per capita sales in jewelry stores declined by 19% from 1983 to 1993. The department stores, both discount and traditional, have cut into the sales of traditional jewelry stores. They all sell gold chains, watches, small gem stones and other items carried in jewelry stores. Also, the membership warehouse clubs sell some larger gemstones and other expensive items such as Waterford crystal and Hummel figurines. They do not have a large selection, but they sell enough to affect the jewelers' market share.

Grocery Stores

At first glance, it does not seem realistic that the per capita expenditure in grocery stores in a state could go down by over 14% in 10 years. Some of this has been caused by the extreme competition among retail chains. But some of it is loss of sales to discount general merchandise stores and membership warehouse clubs. The biggest losses to grocery stores, though, are to restaurants as people continue to eat out more and more. Figure 3-13 indicates that overall, state residents spent $129.6 million less in grocery stores in 1993 compared to 1983. Much of the non-food items previously bought in grocery stores are now bought in discount department stores.

Drug Stores

Iowan's per capita expenditure in drug stores decreased by 10.9% in the 10 year period. Considering that nearly every new discount department store has a pharmacy, and many new larger grocery stores have pharmacies, it is surprising that traditional drug store sales were *only* down by 10.9%. Apparently pharmaceutical sales is a growing segment of our economy. Older people are becoming a larger percentage of the population and they tend to be the main consumers of pharmaceuticals. Therefore, the market for pharmaceuticals is growing and can accommodate more competition without hurting existing merchants inordinately.

Auto Parts Stores

Iowans only reduced their per capita purchases in auto parts stores by 9.1% over the 10-year period. These losses were probably light replacement items such as spark plugs, oil filters, air cleaners, light bulbs, oil, etc. Fortunately, auto parts stores carry thousands of specialty parts, not carried in the discount general merchandise stores. In this way, auto parts stores can still attract business from auto repair shops and professional auto mechanics.

Women's Apparel Stores

The per capita expenditures in women's apparel stores declined by only 2.5% from 1983 to 1993. This is quite a contrast to men's wear that was down by 44.4%. Women's wear stores have sustained themselves because of additional sales to women entering the work force and because women's styles change frequently. However, the small decrease is somewhat misleading. Women's apparel stores had sharp increases in sales throughout most of the 1980s but, for the last four years, the sales have begun decreasing, resulting in a net decrease of only 2.5%. The decrease in sales is likely to continue over the next several years because it appears that women's fashions are beginning to become more casual just as men's did. This means that fewer clothes will be bought in specialty women's apparel stores and more will be bought in department stores.

THE CORNELL STUDY (MEMBERSHIP WAREHOUSE CLUBS)

A 1992 study by Cornell University interviewed 460 supermarket shoppers, and surveyed retail and wholesale companies involved in the food industry in New York and New Jersey to catalog their perceptions of membership warehouse clubs. In an early section of the report, they used Food Marketing Institute data to show why the warehouse clubs are such tough competition. The data showed that, on average, the "clubs" sold to customers for 26% less than traditional supermarkets. Most of this difference was due to the fact that clubs had greater operating efficiency (direct shipping, fewer items, fewer employees, etc.) and because of their added income from membership fees. In addition, the data showed that total operating expenses for clubs ranges from 7 to 9% of sales, whereas operating expenses for supermarkets averages 17 to 20% of sales.

In the survey of consumers they found that 65% had shopped in a club at least once. However, they found that only 29% of the respondents were actually club members. It appears that many of those who shop do so with a temporary membership or as a guest of a member.

Demographic Profiles

The demographic profile of club members and non-members as found in this study is shown in Table 3-1. The most likely member would be female between 25 and 55 years of age, with a household annual income of $20,000 to $60,000 per year, with three to four persons in the household, having one or two children under age 18, with two persons employed outside the household. Another interesting point is that over 27% of the members have annual household incomes *above* $60,000 per year.

Travel Time

Figure 3-14 shows that 56% of the members travel 10 to 20 minutes to shop at the clubs, while 16% travel more than 20 minutes to do

Table 3-1 Demographic Profiles of Wholesale Club Members and Non-Members

	Members	Non-Members
Sex		
Female	87.2	80.6
Male	12.8	19.4
Annual Household Income		
Less than $20,000	10.4	25.8
Between $20,001-$60,000	62.4	59.8
Over $60,000	27.2	14.4
Household Size		
1-2 persons	26.7	42.9
3-4 persons	50.4	42.5
Over 4 persons	22.9	14.6
Number of Children Under 18		
No children under 18	40.2	58.5
1-2 children under 18	42.4	30.9
More than 3 children under 18	17.4	10.6
Number of Persons Employed		
No one employed	8.4	20.0
One person employed	34.4	31.2
2 persons employed	41.2	37.3
3 or more persons employed	16.0	11.2
Age		
Under 25	3.8	4.7
Between 25 and 55	79.5	63.5
Over 55	16.7	31.8

Source: Cornell University, 1992

their shopping at the clubs. For non-members, 40% traveled 10 to 20 minutes to shop at a club, while 36% traveled over 20 minutes to shop at a club. This would suggest that most members live relatively close to their clubs, while distance from the club may be an impediment for non-members to join. However, many people regularly drive up to 100 miles one-way to shop at membership warehouse clubs as surveys in various states have found.

Reasons for Non-Membership

Table 3-2 shows the reasons given by non-members in the Cornell Study for not becoming members of clubs. Over a third of the

Figure 3-14 Travel Time to Wholesale Clubs

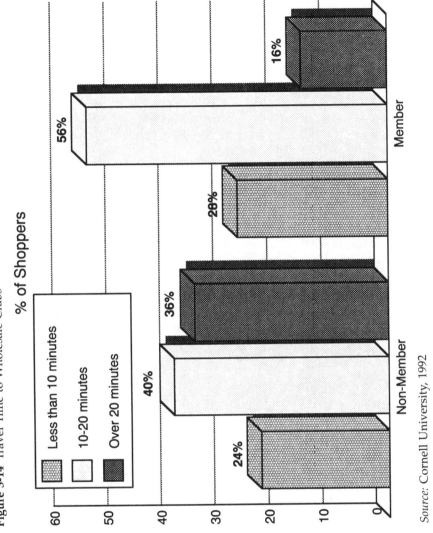

% of Shoppers

Less than 10 minutes
10-20 minutes
Over 20 minutes

56%
16%
28%
36%
40%
24%

60
50
40
30
20
10
0

Member
Non-Member

Source: Cornell University, 1992

Table 3-2 Reasons Given for Non-Membership at Wholesale Clubs

Reason	% of Respondents*
Packs too big--don't want to buy in bulk	35.2
Don't want to pay membership fees	32.9
Prices at wholesale clubs are not better	11.7
Too far--don't like location	11.1
Lack knowledge of clubs	10.7
Don't like product selection at wholesale club	4.4
Shop at wholesale club with friend/relative	4.0
Other	12.0

*Does not total 100% since respondents could give multiple answers
Source: Cornell University, 1992

respondents gave the main reason for not joining as "packs too big/don't want to buy in bulk." Nearly one third (32.6%) said their reason for not joining was that they did not want to pay the membership fees. Surprisingly, 11.7% said they did not join because they believed that the prices at the clubs were not better (than at the supermarkets). Slightly more than 11% of the respondents said they did not join because the club was in a poor location or too far away.

Shopping Perceptions of Club Members

Figure 3-15 shows that a high percentage of members (73%) were satisfied with their shopping experiences at the clubs, compared to 59% being satisfied with their supermarket shopping experiences. But, when it came to truly relish their shopping experiences, 33% enjoyed their supermarket shopping experiences, compared to only 19% who claimed to look forward to their club shopping experiences.

When members were asked about overall value of major departments in a club vs. a supermarket, the majority found better value in the supermarkets in produce, meat, deli, and bakery, as shown in Table 3-3. However, most respondents preferred the clubs to the supermarkets when it came to dry goods, health and beauty care items, and general merchandise.

Figure 3-15 Wholesale Club Members Rate Their Shopping Experience

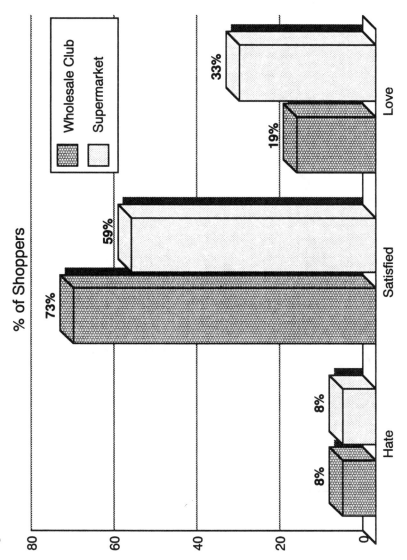

Source: Cornell University, 1992

Table 3-3 Demographic Profiles of Wholesale Club Members and Non-Members

| | % of member respondents rating the format a better value | | | |
	Supermarket	Wholesale Club	Same/ Don't Know	Total
Produce	68.8	10.9	20.3	100%
Meat	59.8	10.2	29.9	100%
Deli	62.5	5.5	32.0	100%
Bakery	54.7	12.5	32.0	100%
Dry Goods	29.5	48.4	22.5	100%
HBC	28.1	43.0	28.9	100%
General Merchandise	18.1	55.9	26.0	100%

Source: Cornell University, 1992

Table 3-4 Club Member Spending and Shopping Frequency at Wholesale Clubs and Supermarkets, by Income Level

| | Annual Income Level ($000's) | | | |
	Below $20	$20-$60	Above $60	All Club Members
Wholesale Club:				
Average $ spent per trip	$71.25	$63.45	$71.45	$66.74
Average # trips per month	1.94	1.62	1.04	1.70
Supermarket:				
Average $ spent per trip	$60.67	$89.40	$102.27	$89.66
Average # trips per month	7.46	7.36	7.94	7.50

Source: Cornell University, 1992

Spending Patterns of Club Members

The Cornell study found that 90% of club members spent less than $200 per month, while only 10% spent more than $200 per month. Conversely, 83% of club members spent over $200 per month in supermarkets and 17% spent under $200 per month, as shown in Figure 3-16.

When looking at amounts spent by annual income level, an interesting pattern shows up. The amount spent per trip is not that

Figure 3-16 Member Spending at Wholesale Clubs and Supermarkets

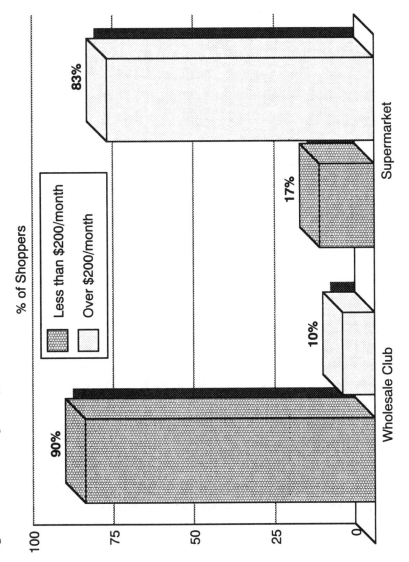

% of Shoppers

Source: Cornell University, 1992

much different for the different income groups. Table 3-4 shows, however, that members with incomes of less than $20,000 shop at the clubs nearly twice as often as those with annual incomes of over $60,000. Yet, the number of trips per month to supermarkets is quite similar, but the lower income consumers spend considerably less per trip. The primary conclusion is that lower income members shopped more often and purchased a higher percentage of their groceries at the clubs than at the supermarkets, compared to the higher income members.

Strategies for Competing

The retailers who were surveyed offered various strategies for competing. Figure 3-17 shows what the retailers believed to be the most effective overall strategies. Their top strategy was to emphasize their service departments. Nearly tied for second place was to emphasize selection and to remodel. They also believed several other things such as reducing costs, adding larger/multi packs, and getting drop shipments were also effective. These strategies seem to work. The grocery chains that have adopted them are usually quite successful. There are no studies to show the impact of the various strategies, but undoubtedly the first three strategies offer the greatest chance for gaining sales.

THE CORNELL STUDY (SUPERCENTERS)

A 1993 study Cornell University, conducted by Gene A. German, Gerand F. Hawkes and Debra J. Perosio, surveyed 300 consumers in Ohio and Arkansas, two markets that have supercenters and other alternative format food stores. Mid-level executives of food manufacturers from across the United States also participated in a written survey, measuring the impact of alternative retail food stores on other stores in their market areas.

Figure 3-17 Most Effective Overall Strategies

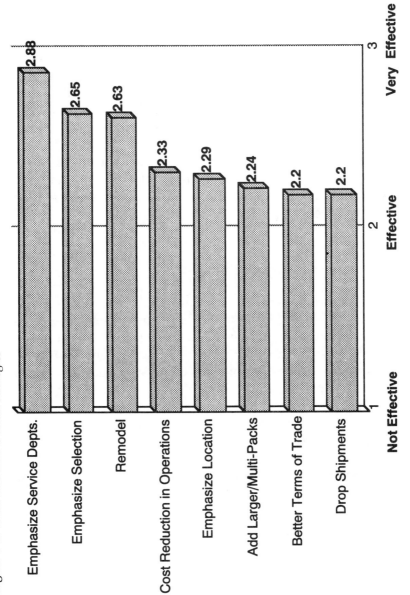

Source: Cornell University, 1992

Changes in Market Shares

A Nielsen Market Research survey of retail sales changes between 1991 and 1992 of major supermarket product categories (292) reported the gains and losses for the different formats. Figure 3-18 shows the percentage of these categories where different retail formats lost market share. As can be seen, the big losers were other food stores with losses in 75% of the categories and supermarkets with losses in 63% of the categories.

On the other hand, Figure 3-19 shows that the big winners were drug stores and mass merchants with gains in market share in 56% of the categories, and other non-food stores gaining in 52% of the categories.

Manufacturer Perspectives

The manufacturers were asked to rank four food retailing formats (supermarkets, supercenters, wholesale clubs, and limited assortment stores) according to five characteristics (price, variety, service level, fresh food department, and well trained employees). Table 3-5 shows their ratings. They ranked the supermarkets first in all categories but price. In perhaps an indication of things to come, they ranked supercenters second in all categories but price. But, when asked to rank the dominance of different formats in the year 2003, the large superstore (over 50,000 square feet) was ranked first, with the supercenter ranked second. The supermarket as we know it today (less than 50,000 square feet) was ranked third.

Consumer Perspectives

Consumers in Ohio and Arkansas were surveyed about their shopping habits and preferences. Figure 3-20 shows that these shoppers, like nearly all others in the country shop more frequently at a supermarket (4.9 times per month, average) than at any other type of store. An average of 3.5 trips were made to supercenters, and 2.3 trips per month were made to mass merchan-

Figure 3-18 Percentage of Product Categories in Which Retail Channels *Lost* Market Share, 1992

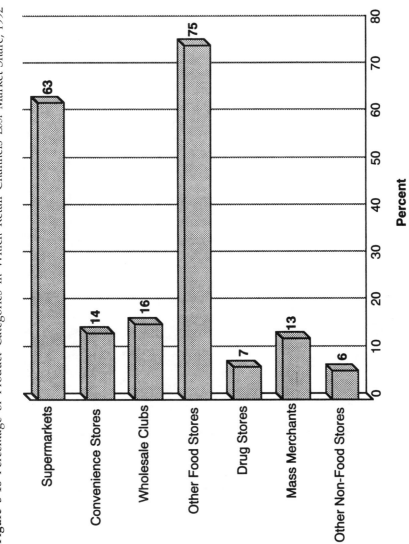

Percent

Supermarkets — 63

Convenience Stores — 14

Wholesale Clubs — 16

Other Food Stores — 75

Drug Stores — 7

Mass Merchants — 13

Other Non-Food Stores — 6

Source: Supermarket Business, March 1993

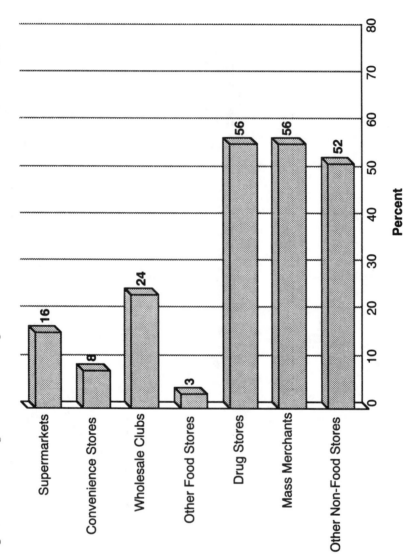

Figure 3-19 Percentage of Product Categories in Which Retail Channels *Gained* Market Share, 1992

Source: Supermarket Business, March 1993

Table 3-5 Competitive Strengths of Selected Food Retailing Formats

Ranking	Price	Variety	Service Level	Fresh Food Dept.	Well Trained Employees
First	Limited Asst. & Wholesale Club	Supermarket	Supermarket	Supermarket	Supermarket
Second		Supercenter	Supercenter	Supercenter	Supercenter
Third	Supercenter	Wholesale Club	Wholesale Club	Limited Asst.	Wholesale Club
Fourth	Supermarket	Limited Asst.	Limited Asst.	Wholesale Club	Limited Asst.

Source: Cornell University survey, 1993

Figure 3-20 Average Number of Shopping Trips per Month at Selected Retail Formats

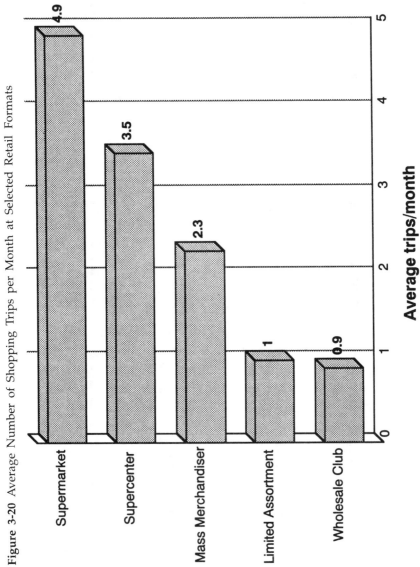

Source: Cornell University Survey, 1993

disers. Table 3-6 shows how consumers spread their purchases over the different format stores. The supermarkets are still the dominant format for food, with 86% of the respondents purchasing. But, when it comes to household supplies, health, beauty care and paper products, more people buy at the supercenters than anywhere else. Consumers also indicated a strong preference for purchasing such perishables as bakery products, deli items, meat and produce at supermarkets.

Figure 3-21 shows the average amount spent per shopping trip by retail format. Again supermarkets lead with $68.93 per trip, followed by supercenters at $59.05, wholesale clubs at $51.01 and mass merchandisers at $32.65.

Table 3-7 shows consumer rates of several characteristics of supermarkets versus supercenters. Supermarkets are ranked higher in every category but low everyday prices and low sale prices. Supercenters were ranked nearly as high as supermarkets in assortment and neat and clean facilities.

ASSOCIATED WHOLESALE GROCER'S STUDY

In 1993, Bill Lancaster, Vice President, Sales for Associated Wholesale Grocers of Kansas City, Kansas, published *Survive & Thrive*, a handbook on competing with alternative stores. In 1994 Mr. Lancaster updated the study and called it *Survive & Thrive II*. He studied the sales of seven local grocery stores that were competing with nearby Wal-Mart Supercenters. He found that after the first three months, their sales had declined by an average of 17%. After three months one of the stores closed, thereby freeing up some market share. The remaining six stores on average gained back 6% of their sales at this point, causing their net reduction in sales to be an average of 11% per store.

SUMMARY

Two rules of thumb can help to identify the impact of mass merchandising on various businesses. *Rule of thumb 1:* Nearby stores selling merchandise that differs from that of the mass

Table 3-6 Percentage of Consumers Purchasing Selected Product Categories at Various Retail Formats

Store Type	Food	Household Supplies	Health & Beauty Care	Paper Products
		Percent of Respondents		
Supermarket	86	50	33	50
Supercenter	57	63	61	51
Mass Merch.	13	37	32	22
Wholesale Club	18	14	9	12
Drug Store	1	5	38	12
Limited Assort.	14	7	3	6

Source: Cornell University Survey, 1993

Figure 3-21 Average Amount Spent per Shopping Trip by Retail Formats

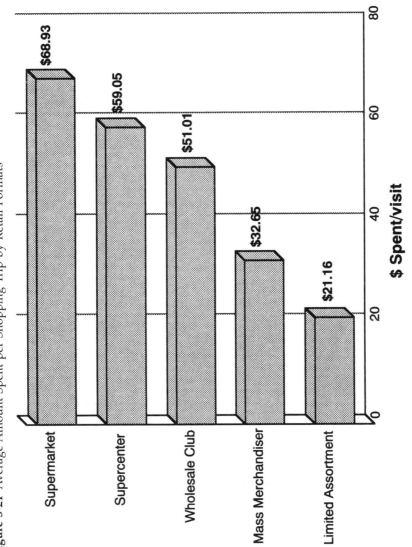

Source: Cornell University Survey, 1993

Table 3-7 Consumer Ratings of Supermarkets and Supercenters on Selected Key Store Attributes

Question: *"We would like you to compare the supercenter and the supermarkets where you shop and tell us which you like better in terms of the following features:"*

	Supermarket	Supercenter	Same/Indifferent
	Percent of Respondents		
Food Quality			
Overall Food Quality	52	22	26
Excellent meat	59	20	19
Excellent Produce	47	27	26
Pricing			
Low everyday prices	30	46	24
Low sale prices	30	44	25
Prices clearly marked	45	23	23
Assortment			
Large assort. brands	39	38	23
Wide variety/selection	39	38	23
Service			
Good checkout service	43	30	27
Friendly atmosphere	44	23	23
Well trained employees	42	25	33
Facilities			
Convenient location	40	30	30
Layout of store	47	26	27
Neat and clean	31	30	39
Pleasing decor	30	37	33

Source: Cornell University Survey of Supermarkets and Supercenters, 1993

merchandiser will probably experience an increase in sales because of a spillover of the additional traffic drawn to the mass merchandiser. *Rule of thumb 2:* Stores selling the same merchandise as the mass merchandiser will probably experience a reduction in sales, since it is very difficult to go head to head with the mass merchandiser.

This could be termed a "zero sum game premise," which applies in many static population areas where mass merchandisers open stores: in essence, the gains in sales by the mass merchandisers will be offset by the losses to existing competing stores, whether they are in the host town or in outlying towns.

The Iowa Study has been conducted every year since 1988 and focused on the impacts of Wal-Mart stores since they came into the state in 1983. In host towns, the study found that general merchandise stores experienced large gains, but when netted out it was primarily Wal-Mart's gain, and many of the competing general merchandise stores suffered reductions in sales. Home furnishings stores in the host towns experienced gains in sales, on average, because most of what they sell is not sold in a Wal-Mart store, and they benefit from the additional traffic drawn to town. Eating and drinking places also benefit from the additional traffic brought into town.

In the non-Wal-Mart towns of the same average population as the Wal-Mart towns nearly every type of store lost sales after Wal-Mart began expanding. The lone category in which the non-Wal-Mart towns had gains in sales was grocery stores. These grocery stores are capturing sales from nearby smaller towns which have lost their own grocery stores.

After Wal-Mart has been in a state for several years, the company reaches a saturation point with some of its stores. Some of the early host towns that experienced an enlargement of the trade area after Wal-Mart opened, later suffered a contraction of the trade area as Wal-Mart stores were placed closer and closer together.

The outlying small towns that do not have Wal-Mart stores were among the hardest hit. On average, the small towns within 20 miles of a Wal-Mart store suffered a cumulative 25% reduction in sales after five years.

The overall buying habits of Iowa residents were studied and it was found that they changed dramatically in the 10 years that Wal-Mart was in the state. The average resident spent nearly 32% *more* in department stores (discount stores) in 1993 as compared to their spending habits in 1983. Conversely, the average Iowan spent 44% less in men's and boy's clothing stores, 31% less in hardware stores, 26% less in variety stores, etc. Studies indicate that these changes occurred because of changes in life styles, the introduction of discount stores such as Wal-Mart and the introduction of "category killer" stores in the cities.

Two Cornell University studies of membership warehouse clubs and supercenters determined consumer's shopping habits and sampled the opinions of business people. The study found that lower income people shop the warehouse clubs more often and purchase a higher percentage of their food at warehouse clubs than at supermarkets. The study of supercenters seemed to suggest that currently most shoppers find their supermarket more attractive than the supercenter when buying perishables. However, it appeared that the supercenter was preferred when purchasing non-perishables. Based on the supercenter growth plans of Wal-Mart and Kmart, the supercenter will be a force to be reckoned with in the future.

A study by Bill Lancaster of Associated Wholesale Grocers of Kansas City, Kansas, indicated that local supermarkets suffer substantial losses of sales in the first few months after a supercenter opens in their area, but gain some of the sales back as some of their cohorts go out of business.

It is clear that the discount mass merchandisers are saturating many market areas and are putting a squeeze on smaller stores. Yet there are many local stores that continue to operate profitably. As will be discussed later, local stores that stick to the basics of doing business and meeting customers' wants and needs can compete on strengths other than low prices and huge selections.

PART II

HOW TO COMPETE

4

IMPROVING YOUR MERCHANDISING

The ability to select the right mix of merchandise, procure it and sell it at the most attractive prices is very important when competing in a mass merchandise environment. Local merchants who once sold a broad selection of goods before the appearance of mass merchandisers, find today that they must reposition their stores and become more specialized in the face of this new competition. This chapter addresses each type of competition and provides you with tactics to improve your merchandising.

COMPETING AGAINST THE DISCOUNT GENERAL MERCHANDISERS

The following tips are offered to merchants who face competition from the discount general merchandisers such as Wal-Mart, Kmart and Target. These types of stores usually are large and have between 30 to 40 departments. Some departments such as children's wear will have a fairly complete selection, but other departments such as plumbing, electrical and hardware will have very limited selections.

Check Out the Competition

The most important action local merchants can take when faced with competition from discount general merchandisers in a market area is to find an existing store of the type announced, visit it and shop it. This seems so sensible, yet it is shocking how few local merchants actually do it. This was driven home to me some time ago when Time Magazine sent a photographer out to shoot some photos for an upcoming story on a mass merchandiser. I was conducting seminars in a small town in Minnesota that had no discount store of its own, but was surrounded by discount stores within a 15 to 20 mile radius. The photographer finally decided to take some shots of me in the local coffee shop seated around a table with six local merchants. Never having met any of these people previously, I faced an awkward situation while waiting for the photographer to set up. In order to break the ice, I asked how many of them had been in the nearby discount stores. To my surprise, not a single person had.

I have told this story on numerous occasions to illustrate the complacency that pervades the thinking of many local merchants, and have since developed a sports analogy to illustrate the foolishness in this attitude. I ask seminar participants if they think that Joe Paterno, coach of the Penn State Nittany Lions football team, would every play another team without first scouting them, reviewing game films, and finding out everything he can about the opposing team. The answer is obviously no and yet we have local merchants who are trying to compete against the top retailers in the world without ever setting foot in their stores. Operating without investigating the competition is truly like operating in a vacuum.

Merchants will often ask, "what should I be looking for when I shop the competition?" There are a number of things that local merchants should look for when shopping the mass merchandisers—for example:

1. Look for voids in the mass merchandiser's inventory mix. Check for brands, models, sizes, etc.
2. Check price points, especially on price-sensitive items.
3. Check out displays, especially end caps and power aisles.
4. Observe signage for benefits and features, price, etc.
5. Observe customer relations practices.
6. Look for checkout procedures.
7. Look at the methods of displaying prices of products.
8. Observe how returns are handled.
9. Observe how customer complaints are handled.
10. Look for policies on matching competitor's prices.

In general, local merchants should look for the mass merchandiser's strengths and weaknesses. Some look only for weaknesses and completely overlook some potential good ideas that they might be able to use. Another practice of local merchants is to shop the mass merchandiser one time and to think that is sufficient for all time. The competing mass merchant should be shopped *regularly.* Mass merchandisers change practices fairly often and if you do not shop them regularly, you will be operating with obsolete information. Even when sports teams play teams they have recently played, they still scout them again to see if they have added any new plays or have changed their defenses.

Some merchants will argue that they simply do not have time to shop the competition. Yes, merchants are very busy people, however, you need to leverage yourself like the mass merchandisers, who usually send their employees out to assist in checking out the competition. Another alternative is to hire professional price checkers.

You could also send employees to competitors' stores to check on the prices of a dozen or so items each week. The chore could be made more exciting by awarding points for finding items that are priced higher in the competitor's stores or for finding voids in the mass merchandisers' inventories. After a certain number of points some worthwhile award could be presented to individuals.

Try Not to Handle the Same Merchandise

It is difficult for small businesses to compete with the mass merchandisers on identical merchandise. Therefore, when possible, owners and managers of smaller businesses should look for suitable alternatives so they can avoid being compared item for item, price-wise. For example, Wal-Mart, Kmart and Target all handle the same brand of incandescent light bulbs. All three companies apparently consider low wattage incandescent light bulbs to be price-sensitive items, and their regular price will be from $1.80 to $2.00 for a four-pack. However, if they are in direct competition with each other, each will try to undercut the other on price. They will often use lightbulbs as "loss leaders," (i.e., selling below their cost) with prices as low as $1.00 for a four-pack of the lower wattage bulbs. I have seen this exact item in local stores priced over $4.00. What do customers feel when they see an identical item priced 400% higher in a local store? Obviously they believe the local store is out to gouge them, when, in fact, the local merchant may simply have marked up the item by the wholesaler's suggested amount or by the store's standard percent.

Higher wattage incandescent bulbs and fluorescent bulbs may be priced higher in the discount mass merchandise stores than at the local stores, and yet customers buy them as though they were the lowest price in town. This shows the great skill of the mass merchandisers in creating a *perception* of "everyday low prices" by being priced very low on price-sensitive items, but taking considerably higher markups on similar items whose price is not so well known. I learned this lesson the hard way, as explained below:

We use 150 watt incandescent bulbs to light the basement of our home. I had been regularly buying them at one of our local discount stores, because I knew they usually had the lowest price in town on the lower wattage bulbs. I had been paying $1.84 for a single 150 watt bulb and thought that I was getting a good deal. One day I accidentally noticed the price of 150 watt bulbs in a nearby grocery store was $1.45, considerably *lower* than the discount store, yet they appeared to be selling very few because their price on the better known low wattage bulbs was considerably higher than at the discount store. This again highlights the importance of using variable pricing where price-sensitive items are regularly marked down to a very competitive level, while higher margins are taken on items whose prices are less well known.

Once, while on a seminar tour to a Michigan town that was getting a new discount store, the manager of a regional discount store across the street from the proposed new store asked if I would walk around his store with him and tell him what my perceptions were. I agreed and he gave me a detailed tour of his store. I made several comments concerning displays, signage, etc. After a while we came to a display of men's denim jeans that were identical to the jeans that Wal-Mart, Kmart and Target sell. The jeans were stacked on a table next to the aisle as though they were on sale, and the sign showed the price to be $15. I asked him if his company would allow him to lower the price. He said no. I asked if the company handled any other brand of comparable quality jeans. He said no. I said, "You have a problem." The new discount store was selling the identical jean at $9.97. (They currently sell the same jean for under $9.00.) What would a customer think, who had just seen the jeans at the discount store for less than $10 and then went across the street and saw the same jean for $15? Most would think, "Wow, this store is selling that jean for 50% more than the discount store." Unfortunately, many customers would then make a gigantic leap in logic and assume that *everything* in the store was priced 50% higher than at the discount store. In most cases that is simply not true.

Some Solutions

If you, as a merchant, feel that you must handle the same merchandise as the mass merchandiser, then it is imperative that the price be no more than 10% to 15% higher, especially on price-sensitive merchandise. If this is an untenable situation and causes the merchant to lose substantial money, then other solutions must be sought.

The most obvious solution is to handle another brand or style. For example, there are several popular jeans that are priced higher than the discount store jeans, yet have a substantial market.

Another solution would be to find a private label jean that sells for an amount similar to the discount store jeans, yet will yield a profit for the merchant.

In the case of light bulbs, there are other brands that have different characteristics. By switching to these other brands, you cannot be compared directly and most consumers would not be as repulsed at seeing higher prices on a different brand.

Some private label merchandise has become so popular that it is thought of by many consumers as name brand merchandise. For example, Craftsman tools sold by Sears Roebuck and Company have become very popular and are favored over other name brands by a large number of consumers, including professionals. Sears' Kenmore brand has achieved nearly the same name brand status. Many of the private label brands handled by the hardware cooperatives have also achieved nearly name brand status. Yet many of these items can be sold for lower prices and still generate a nice profit for the merchant. This is because much of the private label merchandise is produced by name brand manufacturers and the private label is a "knock off" of the name brand. Literally no research and development costs or marketing costs, especially advertising, allows producers to sell the private label items to merchants for a relatively low price, compared to the name brand.

Handle Complementary Merchandise

Most of the discount general merchandise chains have departments which sell a limited selection of fast moving merchandise. This provides a high turnover rate and maximizes the profit per square foot of floor space. However, it is frustrating to customers who are looking for more selection. For example, the discount mass merchandise stores such as Wal-Mart, Kmart and Target carry only a few of the fast moving items in their plumbing, electrical and hardware departments, apparently catering primarily to the light do-it-yourselfers. Consequently, a customer who needs merchandise beyond their limited selection is left frustrated. Therefore, this creates an opportunity for local stores such as the hardware store. Most hardware stores would be well advised to cut back on merchandise in departments where the discount stores have the competitive advantage. For example, traditionally hardware stores have carried housewares, sporting goods, toys, and cleaning supplies, but these are all areas where the discount stores are very strong. Conversely, most hardware stores have a much larger selection of hardware, plumbing and electrical supplies than do the discount general merchandise stores. A good strategy for hardware stores is to lighten up on the merchandise where the discounters are strong, but to strengthen the areas where they have the competitive advantage. The goal is to establish a reputation as the store that has the complete line of plumbing, heating, electrical, etc. The end result is that customers who need anything out of the ordinary, will automatically go to the hardware store because the odds of finding the item would be very good.

Hardware store owners should get to know the discount store personnel and make sure that they know the lines of merchandise carried in the hardware store. The people working in the discount stores are often friends and neighbors, who hold no malice against the local store. In fact it is very common for discount store workers to refer customers to local hardware stores for items not stocked by the mass merchandisers.

Sporting goods stores offer another example of stores that can be repositioned to avoid the strong competition from the discount general merchandisers. Stores like Wal-Mart, Kmart and Target have fairly strong assortments of hunting, camping and fishing merchandise and entry level golf, basketball, football, baseball and soccer equipment. However, these stores usually have gaping voids in their inventory of athletic apparel, athletic footwear and upscale sporting goods. A local sporting goods store would probably be well advised to reduce its inventory of entry level sporting goods and to go more heavily into athletic apparel, name brand athletic footwear and more upscale sporting goods, as well as team sports sales.

One sporting goods store repositioned itself rapidly after a new discount mass merchandiser located within a block of the store. The store owner completely eliminated merchandise where the discounter was very strong. He limited his inventory to apparel, team sports items and every type of athletic shoe known to human kind. In addition, he hired some of the best high school athletes to work after school hours. His business has been booming with no letup in sight.

Consumer electronics store owners feel that by reshuffling their merchandise mix they have been able to continue operating profitably. All the discount mass merchandisers sell low-end 13-inch color TV sets at very competitive prices and most use these items as loss leaders. Therefore, it is very difficult for the local merchant to compete effectively in this environment when often the mass merchant is selling the sets for less than he or she can buy them wholesale. Local merchants have found that it makes sense to give up most of these low end non profit items and concentrate on the higher end sets where the mass merchandisers have less selection and little service, and where the profits are much better.

Some local fabric store owners have found the going tough after discount stores come upon the scene. One of the larger discount general merchandise stores has a formidable fabric department. However, they handle primarily low end merchandise. For example they sell many types of fabric for prices ranging from $3.00 to $6.00 per yard. They also sell two popular brands of patterns for one-half off the regular price. It is extremely difficult for a local fabric store to survive against this competition. Some of the better store operators have repositioned their stores by eliminating the low end fabrics and stocking more fashion fabric and other upscale merchandise, including patterns. It is important to use advertising to inform customers of the store's inventory change.

Get Rid of the Dogs

All merchants at one time or another end up with merchandise that no longer sells. Sometimes the items were purchased when they were a fad. For example, CB radios were extremely popular in the 1970s, but have now given way in most market areas to cellular phones and other wireless devices. In 1977, when I was a new assistant professor at Iowa State University, the University bookstore still had a large selection of slide rules, long after the time when most people had discarded them for portable calculators. Before the time of electronic calculators, slide rules had been indispensable tools for engineers and scientists. The brand and model of slide rule you carried with you was a status symbol. Many of the better slide rules sold for $50 to $100 dollars.

The university book store definitely had held on to their selection of slide rules too long. Finally one day they placed every slide rule in the place in a gigantic dump bin and offered them for sale at $1 each. Even at that savings, they ended up giving some of them away. They had simply "gone asleep at the switch". They should have seen the electronic calculator trend developing and should have started phasing out the slide rules while they could still sell them at a minimum profit.

Merchandise sitting on the shelves is virtually the same as money. When it turns over rapidly, it earns a return on investment through the profits generated. However, when merchandise sits for long periods of time without selling, it becomes a double negative for the merchant. It is not earning a return on investment and, as it becomes more shopworn, it tarnishes the image of the store.

One day while shopping a regional discount store in upstate New York, I came across a section of the Fram oil filter display that stuck out like a sore thumb. Fram oil filter boxes are normally a bright orange color. However, in this section of the inventory the oil filter boxes had faded to a tan color. There could be no doubt in anyone's mind that these filters had been on the shelf for a long time. Upon closer inspection, it could be seen that the dust on the top of the boxes was thick enough to write one's initials. I checked the filter number and found that they were for an automobile that had been *out of production for 20 years*. The image of this store was certainly not enhanced by continuing to carry this obsolete and shabby looking merchandise.

Shelf space in super markets is very valuable. Yet it is quite common to see a super market maintain a four foot section of motor oil that is priced 60 to 80% higher than the discount stores. Convenience food stores can get by selling motor oil for this price since they usually sell gasoline and motor oil is often times added to a car engine at the time it is being re-fueled. Most people go to a super market to buy food and household supplies and most pass up the higher priced motor oil and make a mental note to purchase it the next time they are in a discount store. There are some exceptions to this behavior pattern, but the fact remains that most super markets would be better served by dropping the slow moving motor oils and replacing them with other merchandise that would provide the fast turnovers necessary for profitability.

A humorous example of hanging onto obsolete merchandise well past its time was shown recently on ABC's Good Morning America show. Reporter Steve Fox spent considerable time interviewing the owners of a hardware store that had been owned by four generations of the same family to determine how they were going to compete with the new Wal-Mart store in town. The delightful father (third generation), probably in his 70s was proudly showing Mr. Fox various obscure merchandise that he had for sale in the basement of the store. After showing each item, he would say, "you can't buy that at Wal-Mart. When he finished showing off what appeared to be a 1920s type scythe that was apparently used to harvest grain before mechanical equipment, Steve Fox jokingly asked, "and how many of those have you sold in the last year?" To which the proud shop owner responded, "Well, we haven't sold any, but we've got them if anybody wants to buy one."

The main point here is that *merchandise must move to make money*. When shop owners recognize that they have some "dogs" on their hands, it is imperative that they take steps to clear them out of the store and replace them with merchandise that will provide the required number of turns per year.

Buy Well

Nearly all retailers have the opportunity to purchase merchandise at special values. Most trade shows and many sales people quite often offer special buys. However, some smaller merchants will pass them up because of cash flow problems, shortage of storage space, or other reasons. If possible, merchants should take advantage of these opportunities if the merchandise is something they can sell. When they buy at good values, they can enhance their pricing image plus make a good profit as well.

A variety store in a town of about 3,000 population has been one subject for my studies. The variety store is in the hands of the third generation son. The son married a young lady who is an outstanding retailer. In particular, she is very adept at buying well and at displaying in a very attractive manner. There are no discount stores in this town, but there are Wal-Mart and Kmart stores within 20 miles in all directions. I often find that this local variety store sells merchandise for less than the surrounding discount stores. For example, I once found a popular brand of men's deodorant in this store priced at $1.41 when Wal-Mart and Kmart were selling the same item for $2.38. She was able to under sell the discounters because she apparently had taken advantage of a special buy. However, in such a situation where the discounters were not shopping her store, she should have raised her price to the approximate price of the discounters and then placed a sign near the item showing that her price was lower than the giant discounters. Without the sign, I doubt that many local shoppers recognized the terrific value she was offering. When you offer items for less than the discounter, you have to advertise.

This procedure works fine when your store is some distance from discount stores, but when you are nearby, it is not wise to price below the discount stores. As they shop your store and note your lower price, they will immediately engage you in a price war which you will not win.

Many retailers are also joining buying cooperatives. In effect many of the major hardware and drug store chains are buying cooperatives. The parent company pools the orders of its dealers and then buys in volume to get the best prices. Many of these companies then give patronage dividends at the end of the year based on the volume of purchases of the dealer. These parent companies also provide warehousing, distribution and other services.

Here's an interesting variation of the buying cooperative concept. Dealers are carefully screened by the parent company to make sure that they are financially responsible before they are allowed to become a member. To joint the cooperative they must purchase a specified amount of stock in the company. The company itself has minimal warehousing facilities. Instead they have business relationships with several manufacturers. The dealer members order directly from the manufacturer by phone, fax or mail. The manufacturer drop ships the merchandise directly to the dealer, but submits one consolidated bill to the parent company which it pays promptly.

The parent company, in turn, bills each of its members for its respective purchases in one consolidated statement and expects prompt payment. The beauty of the system is that dealers can get prompt delivery on a huge selection of merchandise and they write only one check for all their purchases. In addition, overhead is kept to a minimum, plus the manufacturers are giving volume discounts. Often these dealers can obtain just as low pricing as the discounters, plus have the flexibility to carry unique merchandise. In addition, there are several regional chains that specialize in categories within categories. For example in the upper Midwest there are large stores that specialize in nothing but hunting, camping and fishing equipment.

Find Your Niche

The primary strategy for most local merchants is to find a niche. It is usually not possible to out-Wal-Mart Wal-Mart or to out-Kmart Kmart, but you can play to your own strengths and to the mass merchandiser's weaknesses. For example, the sporting goods store in a ski area that specializes in ski equipment and apparel has found a niche and will not be bothered by the discount general merchandisers. The fabric store that specializes in fashion fabric and perhaps bridal fabric and accessories has found a niche that will not be infringed upon by discount stores. The upscale children's wear store can usually succeed in a mass merchandise environment since it occupies a niche above its competition.

Table 4-1 provides a quick reference for reviewing merchandising strategies for specific types of businesses that may be competing with discount general merchandise stores.

Table 4-1 Strategies For Competing With Discount Mass Merchandisers

Type of Store	Strategies
Building Materials *Paint, Glass, Wallpaper* *Hardware* *Nursing & Garden Center*	1. Reduce the size of the departments where discounters have the competitive advantage. 2. Strengthen the departments where you have the competitive advanatage. 3. Handle upscale products and different brands. 4. Feature services including expert advice. 5. Focus on specialty areas.
General Merchandise *Department Stores* *Variety Stores* *Misc. General Merchandise*	1. Handle more upscale products. 2. Handle different brands. 3. Focus on specialty departments such as crafts. 4. Look for distribution channels with good buys.
Food *Grocery Stores* *Retail Bakeries*	1. Reduce prices on price-sensitive items handled by the mass merchandisers. 2. Introduce a power aisle as an entry to store. 3. Feature merchandise bought on "deals."
Automotive Dealers *Auto & Home Supply* *Gasoline Service Stations* *Boat Dealers* *Recreational Vehicles*	1. Mark down price-sensitive consumables such as filters, spark plugs, oil & light bulbs to near those of the discounters. 2. Emphasize expert technical advice.
Apparel Stores *Men's & Boys' Clothing* *Women's Clothing* *Women's Accessories* *Children's & Infants' Wear* *Family Clothing*	1. Handle more upscale merchandise. 2. Find niches in specialty areas. 3. Feature alterations. 4. Take special orders.

Table 4-1 Strategies For Competing With Discount Mass Merchandisers *(continued)*

Type of Store	Strategies
Apparel Stores (Cont'd) *Shoe Stores* *Misc. Apparel & Accessories*	
Home Furnishings *Furniture Stores* *Floor Covering Stores* *Draping & Upholstrey Stores* *Radio, Television &* *Electronics Stores* *Computer & Software Stores* *Record & Pre-recorded Tape* *Stores* *Musical Instrument Stores*	1. Emphasize complete selection. 2. Get rid of low end items sold by mass merchandisers. 3. Figure out ways to tap into traffic generated by the mass merchandisers (advertising, bill boards, etc.).
Eating & Drinking Stores *Eating Places*	1. Figure out ways to tap into mass merchandiser's traffic.
Misc. Specialty Stores *Drug Stores* *Liquor Stores* *Wed Merchandise* *Sporting Goods* *Bicycle Stores* *Book Stores* *Stationery Stores*	1. Handle upscale merchandise. 2. Feature complete selections of certain items. 3. Feature personalized service and repair. 4. Feature knowledgable salespeople. 5. Offer 24 hr. prescriptions & free delivery (e.g., especially for drug stores).

Table 4-1 Strategies For Competing With Discount Mass Merchandisers (*continued*)

Type of Store	Strategies
Misc. Specialty Stores (Cont'd) *Jewelry Stores* *Hobby, Toy & Game Shops* *Camera & Photo Supply Stores* *Gift, Novelty, Souvenir Shops* *Luggage & Leather Goods Stores* *Sewing, Needlework & Related Goods*	1. Handle upscale merchandise. 2. Feature complete selections of certain items. 3. Feature personalized service and repair. 4. Feature knowledgable salespeople. 5. Drug stores offer 24 hr. prescriptions & free delivery.
Personal Services *Garment Pressing & Cleaning Agents* *Carpet & Upholstery Cleaning* *Photo Studios, Portrait* *Beauty Shops* *Barber Shops* *Shoe Repair*	1. Primary competition from supercenters. 2. Feature promotional specials on price-sensitive services.
Business Services *Radio, TV, Publisher Representatives* *Photocopying & Duplicating Services* *Commercial Photography* *Disinfecting & Pest Control Services* *Building Maintenance Services*	1. Primary competition from supercenters. 2. Consider leased department at supercenter. 3. Feature experience and technical knowledge.

Table 4-1 Strategies For Competing With Discount Mass Merchandisers *(continued)*

Type of Store	Strategies
Business Services (Cont'd) *Medical Equipment Rental* *Equipment Rental & Leasing* *Prepackaged Computer Software* *Computer Maintenance & Repair* *Photo Finishing Laboratories* *Business Services*	1. Become a service center for mass merchandisers. 2. Consider leased department at supercenter. 3. Feature experience and technical knowledge.
Auto Repair Services *Auto Exhaust System Repair* *General Auto Repair Shops*	1. Feature good values on repetitive services such as oil changes. 2. Hire knowledgable personnel.
Misc. Repair Services *Radio & Television Repair* *Refrigeration Service & Repair* *Watch, Clock & Jewelry Repair* *Re-upholstery & Furniture Repair*	1. Become the repair shop for mass merchandisers. 2. Emphasize experience. 3. Offer guarantee on service.
Motion Pictures *Motion Picture Theatres* *Video Tape Rental*	1. Offer specials on tape rentals.

COMPETING AGAINST THE CATEGORY KILLER STORES

Category killer stores are usually large stores that have a narrow line of merchandise, but have a very large selection. These stores were discussed previously, but include stores such as Home Depot, Builder's Square, Home Quarters, Lowes, in the buildings materials area. They include Circuit City, Best Buy and Silo in consumer electronics. Toys "R" Us is the dominant chain in the toy category. Office Max and Office Depot are examples in the office supply category. Barnes & Noble and Crown Books are examples in the book store business. Hermans and Sports Authority are examples of large sporting goods stores. In pet supplies, PetSmart and Pet Stuff are rapidly expanding.

These large category killer stores locate primarily in cities, because a large population base is required. Consequently, local merchants in those cities may suffer a substantial reduction in sales. In fact, the category killer stores have such great drawing power that they can also impact merchants in smaller outlying towns within a considerable radius.

When competing against the *category killer* stores, many of the same principles used in competing against the discount general merchandise stores still apply. However, some principles are different; these are discussed in the following sections.

Handle the Fastest Moving Merchandise

When competing against a category killer store in your community it will be very difficult to handle different merchandise, since the category killers have a very complete selection, as contrasted to the discount general merchandisers that often have limited selections. You probably know your market better than the mass merchandiser, so here is the chance to get rid of those dogs you have been handling and go for the fast moving, convenience oriented items. Let the category killer store handle the slow moving merchandise. Focus on the customer who wants to get in and out of a store in a hurry.

Offer to Get Out-of-Stock Merchandise

By going to the fast moving merchandise, you run a higher risk of not having merchandise in stock than if you were more of a full line merchandiser. You can still save many of these sales, however, by always offering to acquire the merchandise for the customer in the fastest possible manner. This may mean having a reciprocal agreement with other merchants in the area or an arrangement with a local wholesaler. It almost certainly will mean having relationships with major distributors who can get merchandise to you quickly. In some cases, it may even mean purchasing the item at the mass merchandiser and re-selling it to the customer as a matter of convenience.

Table 4-2 lists some of the typical category killer stores with which you may be competing. It also summarizes merchandising strategies that may be appropriate in such cases.

QUALITY COMMITMENT STEPS TO BETTER MERCHANDISING

To improve your merchandising make the following quality commitment steps.

1. **Make a commitment to check out the competition more often.** Figure out which merchants do the best job of shopping the competition. Look for the good and the bad. Get your employees involved in helping to make these assessments. When you find voids in the competition's inventory, consider filling those voids by handling that merchandise in your store. When you find the competitor out-doing you in certain areas, figure out how you can do it even better than them.

2. **Make a commitment to handle complementary merchandise.** Be willing to give up some of the merchandise that the mass merchandisers are selling more effectively. However, find their weak areas and handle merchandise that

Table 4-2 Strategies For Competing With Category Killer Stores

Type of Store	Typical Mass Merchandisers	Strategies
Building Materials Paint, Glass, Wallpaper Hardware Nursing & Garden Center	Home Depot Builder's Square Home Quarters Lowes	1. Focus on fast moving merchandise. 2. Focus on convenience items. 3. Get rid of slow moving merchandise. 4. Feature special order and quick delivery. 5. Offer installation.
Automotive Dealers Auto & Home Supply Gasoline Service Stations Boat Dealers Recreational Vehicles	Western Auto Pep Boys Auto Zone	1. Focus on convenience items. 2. Offer special order. 3. Offer quick delivery. 4. Offer promotional prices on price-sensitive items.
Apparel Stores Men's & Boys' Clothing Women's Clothing Women's Accessories Children's & Infants' Wear Family Clothing Shoe Stores Misc. Apparel & Accessories	Marshalls T.J.Maxx Ross stores Burlington Coat	1. Hire knowledgeable tailors. 2. Focus on latest styles. 3. Offer special order as a feature. 4. Carry more name brands.
Home Furnishings Furniture Stores Floor Covering Stores Draping & Upholstrey Stores Radio, Television & Electronics Stores Computer & Software Stores	Ikea Lechters Linens 'n Things Bed, Bath & Beyond	1. Handle fast moving items. 2. Get rid of slow moving items. 3. Offer fast service special order. 4. Feature planning and design.

Table 4-2 Strategies For Competing With Category Killer Stores *(continued)*

Type of Store	Typical Mass Merchandisers	Strategies
Home Furnishings (Cont'd) *Record & Pre-recorded Tape Stores* *Musical Instrument Stores*		
Misc. Specialty Stores *Drug Stores* *Liquor Stores* *Gen Merchandise* *Sporting Goods* *Bicycle Stores* *Book Stores* *Stationery Stores, etc.*	Phar-Mor Toys "R" Us Office Depot Circuit City Sports Authority	1. Concentrate on convenience items. 2. Handle fast moving items. 3. Get rid of slow moving items. 4. Offer to special order. 5. Offer quick delivery. 6. Offer repair and service.

will position your store as having a complete inventory of that merchandise.

3. **Make a commitment to get rid of slow-moving merchandise.** Get everybody in the store involved in determining what "dogs" you have in your inventory. Figure out a way to have a clearance sale to get rid of them. Also figure what merchandise you can replace them with to generate the necessary turns to make a profit for you.

4. **Make a commitment to take advantage of any special buys you may come across.** Look for any cooperative buying opportunities. Use these special buys to enhance your pricing image and to increase your profit margins.

5. **When competing with the category killer stores, handle the fast moving merchandise.** Let the category killer stores handle the slow moving items.

6. **When competing with the category killer stores, find ways of getting out-of-stock merchandise for customers quickly.**

5

REVIVING YOUR MARKETING PRACTICES

Marketing is the area of retailing where most merchants are weakest. The term marketing means different things to different people. In retailing, think of it in terms of the following:

- Identifying the demand for goods and services
- Arranging to supply them at competitive prices
- Presenting the merchandise in an attractive manner
- Promoting merchandise
- Taking care to ensure customer satisfaction after the purchase.

Poor marketing practices can foster bad reputations that are difficult to remedy. However, through hard work and dedication, merchants can revitalize marketing practices and improve sales considerably. This chapter presents some practical solutions.

KNOW YOUR MARKET

It is amazing how few business people around the country are truly knowledgeable about the demographics of their trade area. When audiences across the country are asked whether they know what percent of the households in their market have annual disposable incomes of less than $20,000, the majority will vastly underestimate this figure. Many will estimate the percentage to be 10% to 15%, when the number is often as high as 30% to 50%. In general they seem to believe that there are many more higher income households than actually exist. In checking the merchandising mix of many of these stores it is clear that many merchants have positioned their stores *well above* what the majority of the market can afford.

Querying of a similar nature about the age of the market area population typically indicates that merchants also underestimate the numbers of older people. In fact, many merchants do not consider the older population as being significant enough to pursue. This segment of the populace offers exceptional business potential, since it is the fastest growing part of our society. Their incomes vary just like the rest of the population. Many have special needs that are not currently being satisfactorily met. There are many opportunities for merchants who are willing to meet these needs.

One druggist for example has found a niche with older senior citizens who have trouble getting around. Several of these customers purchase merchandise such as pharmaceuticals, personal care items and household care items averaging $200 per month from his store. They could purchase the merchandise for less money from one of the local discount stores, but the druggist offers free delivery to their homes.

How do you get information on demographics for your market area? The primary source is the Census of the U.S. Population. Census information is available in hard copy format at most larger libraries, on computer disks, CD ROM and by some on-line computer services. In addition, several service companies will supply data tailored to your specific needs. The data can also be found in college and university libraries, chambers of commerce, city offices, Small Business Development Centers, etc.

Using U.S. Census Information

The Census of the U.S. Population is conducted every 10 years (most recently in 1990) and contains very detailed information for your market area right down to the city block level. It takes the Census Bureau two years or so to process each census, so the data can be more than two years old before it is published. However it is still the baseline data upon which additional models and estimates are made.

It can be a lengthy process, however, to assemble an analysis of one's retail trade area. First the trade area must be delineated. In other words, the dimensions of the trade area must be established. For example, a simple method would be to assume that the trade area extends in a circular fashion around the business, say a 15 mile radius. A more realistic delineation would assess the competition from competing towns and would end up defining the trade area. For example, the trade area might extend 15 miles to the north, 20 miles to the west, 10 miles to the south, and 10 miles to the east.

The problem in compiling the study comes when one starts adding up the data from the various segments of the trade area. The complete census tracts (several blocks) are simple to add, but where only a part of a census tract is included, an estimate of the percent of the tract that lies within the trade area parameters is required. All this can be done, but it requires a lot of time and patience.

It is much easier to compile a demographic study of one's trade area by merely contacting a marketing consulting company (usually via an 800 telephone call). After supplying the consulting firm with the parameters of the trade area, their computer model quickly compiles the report and often it can be faxed or mailed within a short time, even within hours. Some of these services have extended their analyses to include estimated potential sales for your type of store or product for your trade area. Such an analysis will give a detailed breakdown of the population by age and income. In addition it will include information about occupations, automobile ownership, home ownership, ethnic background, etc. Some astute merchants regularly acquire this information and use it religiously in fine tuning their merchandising mix. They swear it gives them an edge over their competitors.

Focus Group Studies

Regardless of how well merchants know the demographics of their market area, most do not know how customers really feel about their stores. Focus group interviews or consumer image studies can be extremely useful in determining the customers' perception of a store. As a part of our extension program at Iowa State University, we have been performing these studies for more than three decades. We typically enlist 15 to 20 merchants who want to know what customers think about their businesses. We then estimate the costs involved and divide them among the merchants.

The facilitator works with merchants and service organizations to choose four or five diverse groups of eight to ten persons each. For example the groups could be newcomers to town, old timers in town, farm families, ethnic groups, commuters, etc. We rely on the merchants for customer lists. The facilitator then works with the service clubs to help choose people on the merchant lists who may be members of the service clubs. We look for honest, fair, and discreet people. Once the potential candidates are listed, the service clubs make contact with them and attempt to recruit them to participate in a two hour focus group session. The merchants sometimes provide a nominal honorarium to the participants for their cooperation. This may consist of a gift certificate from one of the stores.

The names of the participants remain anonymous and their conversations are recorded on audio tapes which are later transcribed. By keeping the participant's names and conversations anonymous, the participants are much more likely to be open and honest about their perceptions of stores.

Prior to the meeting, the interviewer has classified the list of sponsoring businesses into merchandise categories. For example,

Ann's Fashions, City Women's Wear, and Jane's Boutique would be classified as women's wear stores. The interviewer then leads each group of eight to ten people through a series of questions concerning the different types of businesses. For example he or she might ask the group where they usually purchase women's clothing. Those who respond that they purchase out of town will be further questioned as to why they purchase out of town. The interviewer will then ask group members about shopping at each of the sponsoring stores: what they like, what they dislike, what they recommend, etc. Group members are much more forthcoming with details in this setting than they would be on a written questionnaire. Generally, there are counter balancing comments. For example, if one person recounts a bad experience in a store, others will tell of a good experience in the same store.

After the interviews, the audio tapes are transcribed. The interviewer then consolidates the comments made for each business and makes appointments of 20 to 30 minutes with each sponsoring merchant for briefings about the interviews. The interviewer usually reads the comments verbatim to the merchant. At the end the interviewer answers questions from the merchant and discusses the meaning of the comments.

Merchants are able to make more meaningful changes based on the information they receive from these focus group studies than any other effort undertaken at Iowa State University. For example, in one town, many people complained about the local bakery. The consensus was that the cakes were too dry and that the donuts were too greasy. Some people said they were embarrassed to serve the cakes at wedding anniversaries or birthday parties, and that guests would eat a bite or two and throw the remainder in the trash. But, most also noted that they did not complain to the middle-aged couple who were trying to make a go of the bakery, because they "are such nice people." When these comments were recited to the owners of the bakery, they were shocked. They had no idea that so many people were dissatisfied with their products. The husband suggested that "maybe that is the reason that our business has been down so much." They were referred to bakery experts who helped them with their recipes, and their business improved remarkably.

In another case, several people complained about a local nursery. Their comments indicated that while the owner knew everything there was to know about horticultural practices and diseases of plants and trees, he was too often working with the green goods in the rear of the store and would not come to the counter to help them solve their problems. When we told this to the owner, he was very defensive and said something like "don't they know that I have work to do back there. I don't have time for customers." We helped the owner to see the folly of his remark, and to see that he had important talents that attracted customers, if he would just make himself available. After thinking the situation over, he finally trained a person to help out with the tasks in the rear of the store, and he spent more time assisting customers in the front of the store.

EXTEND YOUR OPENING HOURS

If local merchants are serious about competing in a mass merchandising era, they have to get serious about store opening hours. Unfortunately, this is a major problem across America. For some unknown reason, vast numbers of merchants have slipped into the rut of closing their stores at 5:00 to 5:30 p.m., and not opening on Saturday afternoon or Sunday. This is not satisfactory for large numbers of shoppers. Life styles have changed dramatically in the last generation or two. For example, there exists a high percentage of two income families in which both spouses work outside the household. Various other household configurations exist, including single person housesholds and single parent households where household members are working during the normal work day and cannot shop at stores that are only open from 8:00 a.m. to 5:30 p.m. When merchants refuse to stay open during the hours convenient for consumers, they are in effect saying to the mass merchandisers, "here is about 40% of my potential business that you can have for the taking because I'm not willing to make any effort to get it."

Once merchants gain the reputation of having inappropriate operating hours, it is difficult to extend store hours and convince consumers that you are serious about it. Typically it takes a lot of advertising to get the word out. Consumers have seen so many false starts on extended store hours that they have become somewhat skeptical. Merchant groups across the country have contributed to this by their actions. For example, in downtowns all across America, the following scenario—or a similar one—has been played out time and time again over the last few decades. It usually begins with a group of merchants from a downtown or a strip shopping center deciding that they need to stay open until 8:00 p.m. one night a week. In reality only 15% to 20% of the merchants actually agree to stay open until 8:00 p.m. on a given night. They do not advertise the new hours enough and after about two months they conclude that "it's not working," and so they end the experiment.

After one or two years, another group of merchants may get together and decide that they need to stay open one night a week. The reasoning usually goes, "we tried Thursday nights last time and that didn't work, let's try Friday nights this time." Again 15% or 20% of the merchants try staying open on Friday nights. As before, little attention is given to advertising the fact, and after two or three months, the merchants again conclude, "it's not working," and they return to their regular store hours. What these merchants do not seem to understand is that after years of staying open only during "normal" business hours, it is difficult to convince customers in two or three months that they are now serious about extended opening hours.

If local merchants are serious about extended opening hours, it is essential for at least 40% to 50% of the merchants in a shopping area to have an "iron-clad" agreement that they will cooperate in the extended store hours and further, that all will agree to try it for *one full year*. In addition, the agreement should mandate that the extended opening hours will be promoted extensively during the first year. There is a better synergy created when a greater number of merchants participate: when customers visit one store to shop, they will often spill over and purchase things from other stores. Your advertising efforts help their business, and vice versa.

In spite of the evidence that shopper's life styles have changed dramatically in the last generation or two, many local merchants steadfastly refuse to participate in extended opening hours. Recently, I spoke at a horticultural conference in Miami. I was followed on the program by a greenhouse operator who had requested to speak on the subject, "Who's Afraid of the Discounters?" He claimed that he and his partner were doing well in spite of competition from some new discount stores, and in spite of the fact that they were located 16 miles outside of the major town in the area.

When an audience member asked what his opening hours were, he said that he and his partner could not agree on what they should be. He said that he preferred to stay open until 8:00 p.m. during the growing season, but his partner wanted to close at 5:00 p.m., so they compromised by closing at 5:30 p.m. during the growing season, and closed down completely during the off season. "We stick by those hours too," he said. He then gave an example. He told of how one evening during the growing season, just as he was locking the door at 5:30 p.m., a man came driving up in his car. The man said something like "oh, I'm glad I caught you, I drove 16 miles from town to buy some plants and supplies." The owner replied, "I'm sorry but when we say we close at 5:30, that's what we mean. And by the way, I'm glad that you noticed that it is 16 miles out here, because the next time, you can leave in time to get here before we close." The audience was so stunned, they could not believe what they had just heard. In retailing, there is no place for this kind of inflexibility.

Some Wal-Mart representatives once shared a story about opening hours at a recent conference. They told of how an older couple entered a Wal-Mart store in a summer resort area on a Sunday evening just at closing time. Even though the store was about to close, they were welcomed into the store and they proceeded to the plumbing department. They had just arrived in town to open up their summer home, but found that they had no water because the plumbing had frozen during the winter. Wal-Mart did not have the parts needed to make the repair. At this point, after closing hours on a Sunday evening, many employees would have said, "I'm sorry, we do not have the parts . . . good luck." However, according to the Wal-Mart representatives, the store associate got on the phone and made several calls trying to locate the needed parts. He finally tracked down a plumber who had the parts, and made arrangements for him to meet the couple back at their summer home. This is an example of going the "extra mile" in order to help a customer and stands in stark contrast to the greenhouse owner who refused to even open the door. You can bet your life that this couple will shop at Wal-Mart again.

IMPROVE YOUR RETURNS POLICY

Most of today's consumers have been spoiled rotten by the mass merchandisers. They know that they can take virtually anything back that they purchased from a mass merchandiser and get the item replaced or get their money back. My brother tells of two experiences he had with returns at Wal-Mart. He and his wife have a large family, and one Christmas the children gave their parents an electric mixer they purchased at Wal-Mart. After a few months, the mixer quit working. My brother took the mixer and the cash register receipt to another Wal-Mart store (not the one where it was purchased). With very few questions asked, store personnel cheerfully gave him not only another mixer, but also five dollars and some change in addition. When my brother asked what the money was for, the Wal-Mart associate explained that the item had been reduced in price since he had bought it, so the money was for the balance. My brother said he felt like he had come across "money from heaven," and he joked about going home and looking for other things purchased at Wal-Mart that might now be lower priced.

One Good Return Gives You a Customer for Life

The other story my brother often tells involved his youngest son. About four years ago, my brother purchased two telephone answering machines at Wal-Mart. One of them never did work right, but he never got around to taking it back. Last year his son went off to college, he took the defective answering machine with him, thinking that he could fix it. However, he could not find the problem. On the off chance that they would be able to help, he took the machine to the local Wal-Mart store and told the associate that his father bought the machine at a Wal-Mart store over four years ago and it has never worked right. The associate informed my nephew that Wal-Mart no longer sold the item, but he looked the item up in a catalog and noticed that they did sell that item a few years ago and it sold for around $50. The associate then refunded the purchase amount to my nephew and he found a new answering machine at Wal-Mart for $40. He will probably be a Wal-Mart shopper for life.

The above stories can be contrasted with a situation I witnessed in South Dakota a few years ago. During a break at one of my seminars, a local physician confronted a local hardware store owner. He complained that he bought a string weed cutter last May for $140. He said he took it home and it didn't work, so he brought it back to the hardware store, only to have the store's employees tell him that the only thing they could do was to send it back to the manufacturer to have it repaired. The physician said that he did not get the weed cutter back until August. During the time he needed it the most, his cutter was back at the factory. "What kind of way is that to do business?" he asked. The store owner's response was, "I'm sorry, I was not aware of the situation." I think the physician had a valid complaint; that is a terrible way to do business. A good hardware store would have loaned the doctor another weed cutter while his was being repaired.

Another situation emphasizes the difference that a good returns policy can make. I had purchased a name brand facsimile machine from a local dealer. After a few months it quit working. I took it back to the dealer the next morning, and around noon of that day, the service department called me and said, "Your machine has something seriously wrong with it and we cannot fix it here. Unfortunately, we do not have one in stock, either. But if you call the company's toll free number in Corvalais, Oregon, they will take care of you." Dubiously, I made the call. The gentleman who answered, asked about the problem, and took some customer information from me. His immediate response was, "I will send you a new machine by overnight express and you should receive it by noon tomorrow. When you receive the new machine, put the old machine in the shipping carton and send it back to us at our expense. I was still skeptical. But, sure enough, by noon the next day, the new machine arrived. I sent the old machine back at their expense and I will be a confirmed customer of this company for the rest of my life.

The "Credit Only" Trap

Another problem with many local merchants that is all too common is the "credit only" syndrome. This refers to merchants who will take back merchandise that customers return but will not give cash refunds. Usually customers have valid reasons for asking for cash refunds for returned merchandise. Sometimes they have received the item as a gift and they cannot find anything else in the store that they want. Sometimes the colors or styles of an item are wrong when they actually get it home. There are many other valid reasons for asking for a cash refund. My wife Jan and I ran into such a situation a few years ago. I had purchased a pair of jogging shoes for her at a local sporting goods store. When she tried them on they did not fit. Jan and I went back to the store and tried on every pair of jogging shoes in her size, but nothing fit well. By that time, we were both exasperated and I told the manager, "I guess we'll just take the money back." To which he replied, "I am sorry, all I can do is give you a credit." After a serious discussion over the matter, he reluctantly agreed to give us a refund.

A local merchant's return policy must be comparable to that of the mass merchandisers. Customers have come to expect hassle-free returns and when they are hassled over a return they become upset, and many will quit doing business with the offending store.

What to Do with Problem Returns

It is true that some customers do take advantage of merchants. Owners of women's wear stores will tell of the woman who purchases a cocktail dress, wears it to a special party and then tries to return it, claiming that it had not been worn. In another case, youngsters found a way to tear their expensive athletic shoes after they have become somewhat worn. They then return the shoes to the store claiming a defect and receive a new pair of shoes. Other merchants tell of scoundrels who steal merchandise at one store and take it back to another store that handles the same brand and get a cash refund. Dozens of similar stories can be told.

These are difficult situations and place the merchant in a dilemma. How should returns be handled? First of all, it is perfectly acceptable to display a sign indicating that returns must be accompanied by some proof of purchase. Secondly, a merchant should give the customer the benefit of the doubt. For example if there are no *obvious* signs that a garment has been worn, do not make an issue of it. If a defective item has a factory warranty replace the item for the customer and request the manufacturer to honor the warranty. In other words, do the best you can to please the customer. One merchant tells me that he does whatever it takes to make the customer happy, with respect to returns. He said "sometimes when it hurts me too much, I just write it off as advertising. I think it is some of the most effective advertising I do, because then the customer is out telling how great he or she was treated rather than how lousy they were treated."

There is an old saying in retailing that it takes five times as much money to get a new customer than it does to keep an existing one. It's true. There is a limited supply of new customers available, and it takes a lot of advertising and promotion to even get them into the store. I once saw a sign in the back of a store that said, "It takes months to get a new customer, but only seconds to lose one." This sign should be posted in every retail store in North America.

SHARPEN YOUR PRICING SKILLS

It is my contention that many local merchants get a "bum rap" concerning their price levels. Many customers believe that local merchants sell at higher prices than they really do. Why do they believe this? Because in many cases, consumers do not know the going price on more than a few hundred items. They tend to know the prices of items they buy most frequently, the things that irk them to have to buy, or goods that are seasonal or that they have seen advertised frequently. For example, people who do grocery shopping tend to know the price of commonly consumed items such as meats, bananas, soft drinks, paper products, health and beauty care items, milk, bread, disposable diapers, etc. Consequently, when they shop a new grocery store to decide if they want to switch to it, they make judgments based on the *few items that they know the price of.* If upon entering a store they see bananas priced at 80 cents per pound, two liter name-brand soft drinks at $1.75, milk at $3.00 per gallon, 175 count Kleenex at $1.55; what price image starts building up in their mind? Probably they would think "this is a high priced store, because these items are 40% to 100% more than they are at my regular store." However, if they had bought an entire cart of groceries and compared the prices overall, they might find little difference.

A colleague recalled such a situation. He shopped at a store in my town that most people regarded to be the lowest priced store in town. This perception came about primarily through the advertising efforts of the store. Twice a week they placed lengthy, well done circulars in the daily newspaper. These circulars focused on highly price-sensitive items marked down to a very attractive price. Conversely, the supermarket where I shopped was perceived by many people as being the highest priced store in town. This reputation was probably brought about because the store advertised very little, but instead relied primarily on in-store specials. My store was particularly negligent in marking down price-sensitive items, but instead, apparently took some type of standard markup on most merchandise. My colleague said one weekend, he and his wife forgot to do the shopping for an upcoming visit by relatives (his store closed at 8:00 p.m. on weekdays and closed completely on Sunday). He reluctantly went to the store where I shopped (which stayed open until midnight seven days a week). He said his heart sank when he entered the store and he encountered bananas at 75 cents a pound when he had been paying 40 cents a pound at his store. He encountered other items that were lower priced at his store and he said he was very dejected as he rolled his overflowing cart up to the checkout lane. He saved the cash register tape and when his store opened again he made a special trip to check the price on every item he had bought at the "high priced" store. He said he couldn't wait to get home to tally up the figures and demonstrate to his wife how smart they were for shopping at their lower priced store. After arriving home, he quickly added up the figures and was shocked to find that the price totals for the two stores came within pennies of each other. My friend had an inaccurate perception of the pricing structure of the two stores based on the several price-sensitive items for which he knew the price.

I encountered a similar situation a couple of years ago. I was scheduled to speak before an association of farm supply stores. To prepare for the seminar, I shopped one of their stores. When I entered the store there was a pyramid-shaped display of name brand motor oil just inside the front door. A large sign boasted, "sale, $1.49 per quart." At the time, most of the local discount stores were selling the same oil for around 95 cents per quart. My first impression of the store was, "Wow, this is a high priced store." But as I continued deeper into the store, I came across a halogen composite headlight like the one I had just replaced in my three-year old car. It was priced at $7.50, whereas I had paid $12 for my replacement at a well known discount chain. As I continued to look around the rear of the store, I found several more items priced lower than at the local discount stores. I concluded that this store had some terrific bargains, but they threw me off on my entry to the store by pricing a price-sensitive item much too high. Other customers might not have ventured past the front door after encountering such a price shock.

On the other hand why do most people perceive that discount stores are lower priced on most merchandise? In fairness to the discount stores, most of them do have a lower mark-up as indicated by the gross profit margin on their operating statements. However, they are also masterful at *variable pricing*. For example, the top discount mass merchandisers carry approximately 70,000 to 80,000 items or stock keeping units (sku's) in their larger stores. However, it is commonly believed that they treat only 500 to 600 of these items as price sensitive. In other words, these are the items for which they are shopping the competition to compare prices. If lower prices are encountered at a competitor's store, at least two of

the top companies have authorized their store managers to immediately mark their prices below those of the competitors.

Meanwhile, the discount stores are very adept at knowing
which items of merchandise they can take larger markups on. A
good example is incandescent light bulbs. As was described
previously, most discount stores consider the four pack soft white
bulbs to be very price sensitive. One of the top chain's regular price
is $1.84, but if they get into a price war with one of their
competitors, they have been known to mark the price down to as
low as a dollar, when local merchants often sell the same four pack
for around $4. At the same time, the higher wattage bulbs (which
are sold as singles only) are apparently not considered price
sensitive by the discounters. I use 150 watt soft white incandescent
light bulbs in my basement. For some time I had been buying them
at one of the top discount stores for $1.84. I had assumed that if the
discounter was lower priced on the lower wattage four packs, then
they must also be lower priced on the higher wattage bulbs. One
day while shopping in my grocery store, however, I noticed that
their regular price for the 150 watt bulb was $1.45. The discount
store was selling this bulb for nearly 19% more than the local
grocery store, yet I would bet that the discount store sold many
more of these bulbs than the grocery store because of customers
making the same erroneous assumptions that I had made.

Developing Your Pricing Strategy

It is important for local merchants to make a commitment to
variable pricing. The owner/manager should develop a list of
price-sensitive items for his or her store. This list for smaller stores
may consist of only 10 to 15 items. Of course the number would be
higher for larger stores. There are several ways of compiling the
price-sensitive list. A few of the methods are listed below:

- Get the list from a parent company.
- Watch what the discount stores are featuring in their ads.
- Observe what the discount stores are featuring on their end
  cap displays.

- Compile your own list with the help of employees and customers.
- Read trade journals and watch for price comparisons.

Once the list is compiled, the store manager must ensure that major competitors are shopped regularly to find their prices. It is usually futile to try to undercut the prices of the major discount stores, because they will engage in a price war which they will usually win. If you can price your price-sensitive items no more than 10% to 15% higher than the discounters, you will find acceptance among your customers. It is when they start seeing your prices 40% to 400% higher that they notice. However, some local merchants match the discounter's prices to the exact penny. Most of them have found that the discount stores will not engage them in a price war as long they are not underpriced.

The following story illustrates the futility of engaging a major discounter in a price war. A couple of years ago, a fabric store owner in Ohio called me at home. She told me that Wal-Mart had opened a new store in her town and when she checked them out she found, among other things, that Wal-Mart was selling a certain type of popular yarn for less than her price. She said she hunted around and found a special buy on the yarn which allowed her to reduce her price below the Wal-Mart price. She said, however, that the next time she shopped Wal-Mart they had marked the price of their yarn below her new price. She said that she again found another good buy on the yarn, so again she priced the yarn below the Wal-Mart price. Her emotional question to me was, "What do I do now? I have lowered my prices to the point that I am losing money and they are still lower than me." Of course, my response was, "do not undercut their prices."

Display Prices So They Are Easy to Read

In addition to using variable pricing, local merchants need to be bolder and more forthright in displaying the prices of their merchandise and services. Today's shoppers do not have time to play games trying to figure out the prices in a store. They have become accustomed to seeing prices displayed prominently in the mass merchandiser stores. When they cannot find prices in a local store or cannot find anyone to help, they often assume that the item is high priced and just walk out of the store.

I have developed what I call the *bifocal test* with respect to price displays. On a hot summer day a couple of years ago, I decided to check some prices in a Wal-Mart store. As I approached the store entryway, I realized that I had left my eye glasses in my car. I am far sighted and use glasses primarily for reading, so I often forget to take them with me. Once I get inside a store where there is reduced lighting, I can't read much without them. On this particular day, I decided to go on into the store. To my surprise, I could read the prices on virtually *every item* in the Wal-Mart store because they used shelf labelling. Below each item on the shelves was a larger sticker with the bar code and a large black on yellow price (3/8 inches high). Above each hang rack was a similar tag. I later walked down the street to a competitor's store. I could read the prices on very few items, because they did not use shelf and hang tag labelling. Instead, they had placed the familiar small price tags directly on the items. They were very small price tags with weak, small print on them. I would guess that the print was 12 point, which is slightly larger than the letters and numbers in this book. In addition, some of the stickers were placed on the front of the item, some on the back and some on the bottom. The point is that this merchant made it very difficult for older customers with diminished vision and, in fact, made it difficult for all customers to find the prices. More impulse sales can be made when customers can easily see the prices as they walk down the aisles, as compared to not being able to see the prices.

IMPROVE YOUR SIGNAGE

Many local merchants have woefully inadequate signage in their stores in general. In this age of reduced service, consumers have come to depend on signs to inform and educate them. The following is a partial list of the useful functions signs serve in a store:

- Signs show when an item is on sale or marked down
- They indicate a new item in the inventory
- They list the benefits and features of items
- Signs give the directions to the location of various merchandise
- They show the qualifications of store personnel
- Signs communicate the store's policy on:
  —meeting competitor's prices
  —accepting checks and credit cards
  —services such as free gift wrapping
  —delivery or pick up
  —special ordering

Use In-Store Education Displays

Today's consumers are bombarded with an increasing array of new products when they have less time for educating themselves about them. Consequently, many consumers are befuddled about the benefits and features of the products they are trying to buy. Some of the dilemmas that come to mind are:

- What does amperage mean on a vacuum cleaner? Do I need 12 amps or is 7 sufficient?
- What is the difference in a two-cycle and a four-cycle lawn mower engine?
- What is the difference between a one-stage and a two-stage snow blower?
- Do I need a four-ply garden hose or is two-ply sufficient?
- What is a progressive lens in a set of eyeglasses? Is it better than bifocals or trifocals?
- Do I need four bearings in my fishing reel or is two sufficient?
- What is the difference in the fertilizer that sells for $15 per bag and the one that sells for $5 per bag?

Obviously the list could go on and on. Manufacturers sometimes provide product information on the package, however, in this era of environmental awareness, packaging is being mini-mized and with it less chance to explain the properties or benefits and features of the product. Some retailers are noted for their outstanding educational store displays. For example Home Depot, the home building materials store giant, places educational dis-plays strategically throughout their stores. They will display cross-sections of their three or four types of garden hose, and consumers can see sizes of the reinforcing material and can read about the properties of the various layers. Home Depot also will install hinges on cabinet doors with notations of the properties, and encourage customers to test them.

Crate and Barrel, a very successful importer, does a great job of incorporating product information with benefits, features, and prices on tastefully done signs on most of their products. Sharper Image, a store that carries new and unusual gadgets also does an outstanding job of placing informational signs on most items displayed. This is very helpful to consumers who may not be familiar with the item and may not be able to find a sales person to explain things to them.

Buy a Sign-Making Machine

A few stores are blessed with people who are very skillful at making hand-lettered signs. However, most of the hand-lettered signs in stores look amateurish and many are just plain hard to read. A better solution is a sign-making machine. The older machines typically used mechanical methods of printing on stan-dard size stock. The newer generation of sign-making machines use computer technology to generate type and graphics that can be printed on a laser printer or an ink jet printer on various size paper. Most stores have a standard size of paper stock for pricing, sales and other functions. It is good to have a uniform color with the logo printed on it. The newer machines can scan in the logo and/or other graphics such as trade marks or brand logos.

Display price information in a uniform manner at a size that most people can read from three to six feet away. For spe-cial values—such as closeouts, special buys, clearances or markdowns—it is important to place special signs that are larger and more attention-getting than the regular price signs. If you have a "percent off sale," the percentage should be noted in large numbers, but it is also good to note the before price and the sale price. It is also important to place signs at eye level for the average person. This should be in the range of five to six feet off the floor.

USE END CAPS AND POWER AISLES

Merchants across the world have trained customers well over the years to believe that items displayed on end caps or in power aisles are special values. End caps are the racks or shelves on the ends of the regular shelves that face toward the main aisles. Since the main aisles have most of the traffic, merchandise displayed on end caps is exposed to the eyes of many more shoppers than the merchandise in the side aisles. Astute merchants know, and studies have shown, that sales of a particular item can be increased dramatically by placing it on an end cap along with attractive signs. In addition, many merchants use what is called cross merchandising on end caps. For example, in a drug store, an end cap that might be displaying sun glasses may also display sun tan lotion, film and beach sandals, since someone buying sun glasses may very well be heading for an outing where the other items may also be needed. Likewise, a hardware store or home building store that has wallpaper displays on end caps may also have displays of wallpaper paste, brushes, and knives that may be needed in a wall papering project.

The phrase "power aisles" is a generic term for the highly trafficked aisles in a store. Some merchants choose to use these aisles to display special values, seasonal merchandise and/or price-sensitve merchandise. Merchandise placed in these aisles grabs shopper's attention quickly and usually yields higher sales than the same merchandise placed in a side aisle. Some grocery stores compete with nearby discount general merchandise stores by incorporating the power aisle into the entry way of the store. Some call it a *wall of values*. The stores are set so that customers must walk down the wall of values as they enter the store.

Typically this aisle is lined on both sides with price-sensitive merchandise that might otherwise be bought in a discount store. The merchandise is marked down to be at or near the discounter's prices. Most people recognize this and start filling their cart as they enter the store. Many customers, not wanting to travel any further than necessary, will purchase the rest of the items on their shopping list at this store and feel assured that, considering the values they acquired along the wall of values, and the value of their time, they have done about as well as possible and it will not be necessary to make the trip to the discount store.

DEVELOP A SPECIAL ORDERING CAPABILITY

It is impossible for any store to stock everything that customers ask for. However, it is unforgivable to send the customer away by merely saying, "I'm sorry, we do not have that item, have a nice day." At the very least, the customer could be referred to another nearby store that may carry the item. But, an even better solution would be to say to the customer, "I'm sorry, we do not have that item in stock, but I could special order it for you and have it by Thursday." Many sales can be saved in this manner and customers appreciate the service. Many merchants have told me that as much as 30% or more of their sales are special order.

The logistics of special ordering have improved tremendously over the last several years. For example, many wholesalers and manufacturers have computerized their inventory control systems, and can immediately know if the item is in stock. In fact, some wholesalers and manufacturers are providing means for retailers to tie store computers into the supplier's computers to instantaneously check on the availability of merchandise. In addition, fax machines and electronic mail give retailers the potential for quickly ordering and verifying shipment of merchandise. Perhaps the biggest boon to special ordering is the development of rapid delivery, whether by regular freight or by overnight express.

Local merchants should familiarize themselves with their suppliers quick shipment capabilities. They should insist that suppliers without such a capability develop one as soon as possible. Furthermore, merchants should make sure that they stock all the necessary catalogs and ordering forms so that orders can be placed quickly and efficiently. Many merchants are actually setting up catalog centers where merchandise can be displayed and where orders can be placed.

Even larger retailers such as J.C. Penney offer special ordering. In their smaller stores, they do not have room to display all their lines of apparel, but instead have swatch books, where customers can observe and feel the material and then place an order. Home Depot, Builders' Square, and Home Quarters all display signs offering to special order items that are not in stock.

Once while visiting with the owner of a small fishing tackle store, a customer came in and requested a part of the mount on a depth finder that he had purchased at the store. The owner immediately responded that he was out of the part, but that he had two ordered for other customers and he would see if he could get another. He immediately picked up the telephone and called his supplier. The supplier confirmed that it could ship the requested part. The dealer reported to the customer that the part was available and that it would be in tomorrow. The customer was pleased, but stated, "I was in hopes that I could get the part today since I have the day off and had wanted to go fishing." To which the dealer responded, "Well, I do have one new depth finder in stock. I will take the part off it and when the new one comes in I will reinstall it." The customer was ecstatic. He then asked if the owner had been out at the lake. The owner said that he had and that the crappie were biting well over on the north side. The customer really became excited at that point and started asking about lures, etc. In short order, the store owner had sold not only the requested part, but also several lures and other fishing supplies. These sales probably would not have occurred if the store owner had not been willing to place a special order and "go the extra mile" for the customer.

DEVELOP EXCITING AND FUN PROMOTIONS

There are outstanding merchants across the country who are truly innovative in developing promotions to generate fun and excitement for customers. Take, for example, the following case of a merchant in a small town in upstate New York. This man owned a lawn and garden center along with a nursery. Obviously the winter months are slow for this type of business in colder climates. However, this business owner was not content to suffer through the "slow months" without doing something about it. Several years ago he decided to construct displays in celebration of the Christmas and Hanukah holidays. He resurrected some old animated displays that his family had brought from Europe many years before. Included was a nativity scene. Little by little he began incorporating live animals into his offering. For example, he had a mother pig who had several baby piglets. He had a mother sheep with a baby lamb. In addition he had the usual menagerie of donkeys, cows, etc., which became, in effect, a petting zoo. Over the years he has added to the animated displays and the live animals. The end result was that people were coming from miles away to visit his displays. Last year over 75,000 people visited the display, often times led by children, who remembered it from last year.

Of course the owner of the lawn and garden store was smart enough to recognize that when there are 75,000 people walking through your store in a six-week period, there is a great opportunity to sell merchandise. Accordingly, he stocked a complete selection of Christmas trees and set up a sizable area displaying handmade craft items appropriate for the holiday season. In addition he stocked a full line of holiday decorations and included free gift wrapping. Of course, this promotion has boosted his sales tremendously, but it also develops a tremendous amount of goodwill among the local populace. One of the less apparent fringe benefits derived from the promotion is drawing children into the store who then come back as a matter of habit as they grow older and become wage earners.

QUALITY COMMITMENT STEPS TO BETTER MARKETING

1. **Get to Know Your Market.** Figure out the dimensions of your trade area and then go to the library, your chamber of commerce or local college and find out the specifics of the

people living there. If you do not have the time for this, consider contacting a data service company which specializes in demographics. Find the answers to these questions about your customers:

- What is their income?
- What is their age?
- How many own their homes and what are they worth?

Once you get this information, examine it in relation to the merchandise mix in your store. Are you in tune with the tastes and preferences of your market population? Consider conducting a focus group study interviewing diverse groups of customers about their attitudes toward your store. If you see a pattern of complaints, take action to correct them. It is also important to read trade journals and magazines such as *American Demographics* to keep abreast of demographic trends.

2. **Examine Your Store Operating Hours.** Are your hours in tune with the lifestyles of your customers? Are your hours similar to those of the major retail chains in your area? If not, extend your hours so that more of your customers can get to your store at convenient times. Closing at 6:30 p.m. instead of 5:30 p.m. would allow time for some of your customers to shop after work. In some towns, staying open one night a week provides your customers with an opportunity to do some of their shopping at your store. Most mass merchandisers stay open on both Saturday and Sunday. More and more people across the country are doing their shopping on the weekends. Your solution to this problem can bring you extra business, but implementing change is not easy. You will need to make a commitment to the new store hours and promote the change frequently. In addition if you can persuade your retail neighbors to remain open during the same hours, all of you will benefit from the cumulative effect.

3. **Adopt Variable Pricing.** Make a list of the price-sensitive items in your store. Check to see what the mass merchan-

disers are selling these items for and adjust your prices accordingly. Also check their prices on "blind items" and, if you find their prices higher than yours, increase yours to their level. Make a practice of checking the mass merchandiser's prices regularly. Get your employees invovled in price checking so that they too become familiar with the relative price levels.

4. **Improve Your Advertising.** Decide on your top two competitive advantages. Start incorporating them prominently in your advertising. Feature price-sensitive items, seasonal items, and new items in your ads. Try to talk your merchant neighbors into cooperatively advertising to draw more customers to your shopping area.

5. **Develop a No Hassle Returns Policy.** Customers have been spoiled by the mass merchandisers. They expect full satisfaction on returned merchandise. Do what is necessary, within reason, to keep them happy. On occasions when you feel that you were taken advantage of, write it off as advertising. Remember the old adage that it takes five times more money to get a new customer than it does to keep an existing customer.

6. **Improve Your Signage.** Take a good look at the signs you have, both inside and outside of your store. Ask some of your most trusted customers for their opinions on their signage. If necessary, place a new sign with the store name and your competitive advantages in a prominent location outside. If you do not have a sign making machine, consider buying one to make signs for the interior of your store. Train your employees to operate the sign machine. Use machine made signs to announce sale items or mark downs. Consider making benefits and features signs for new items or for items where customers may need assistance in evaluating them. Don't over do your signs, but selectively place them to attract the customer's attention and provide some assistance.

7. **Improve End Caps and Power Aisles.** Re-think how you are using your end caps. Develop a program to display

price-sensitive items, seasonal items, and clearance items in order to enhance the image of your store. Develop attractive signs with large lettering to describe the items and their prices. Especially note the regular price and the sale price and/or the percent markdown. Plan a program to change displays at least every month, if not more often.

If your store lends itself to a power aisle, and you don't have one, think about developing one. A power aisle is a great way to impress customers as they enter your store. For example, a lawn and garden store can line the entry way of the store with flowering plants and shrubs with prices prominently displayed. Most customers are favorably impressed and get into a buying mood. This is quite a contrast to a store that places fertilizer at the store entrance. Power aisles are also good ways to favorably impress customers with prices on price-sensitive items.

8. **Work with Suppliers and Employees to Develop Educational Displays.** Check with your suppliers. Ask for in-store displays or videos, and use them. If you need additional displays, work with your employees to develop your own. For example, if you own a fabric shop, consider sewing a garment from a new fabric, using a popular pattern. Display the garment on a mannequin along with signage indicating the pattern number, fiber content, care instructions and other information.

6

PROVIDING OUTSTANDING SERVICE TO YOUR CUSTOMERS

Most local merchants can provide better and more personalized service to their customers than can the mass merchandisers. However, as time goes on, many mass merchandisers are finding ways to enhance their service capability. For example, Wal-Mart and Kmart usually establish a relationship with a local repair shop to take care of warranty problems for lawn and garden equipment and other items that may require service or repair. They are also incorporating interactive kiosks to assist consumers in answering questions. For example, Wal-Mart has such a kiosk in their automotive department. By using a touch panel screen, customers can identify the part numbers for replacement parts for their vehicles. The computer completes the transaction by printing out the list of items, complete with part numbers.

In addition, outfits such as Home Depot, Builder's Square, and Home Quarters have found ways to deliver merchandise to customers and can arrange for installation of many of the products that they sell. Most of these stores also offer to special order items not in stock. The same goes for the membership warehouse clubs such as Sam's where they display signs and catalogs to encourage customers to special order items (such as commercial office furniture) when it is not in stock. Nevertheless, most small businesses can offer these and other services in a more responsive and personal manner than can the mass merchandisers.

EMPHASIZE EXPERT TECHNICAL ADVICE

In the vast majority of discount general merchandise stores around the country, it is difficult to find anyone who knows the merchandise well enough to explain it to a customer. Most of the people working in the aisles of these businesses are primarily stockers who pick up merchandise in the stock room and place it on the display shelves. Conversely, many people working in smaller local stores know quite a bit about the merchandise. This is a tremendous advantage for the smaller merchants since large numbers of customers do not know much about items that they seek to purchase. They desperately search for information on the technical and operational aspects of items they want to purchase.

For example, when my wife and I first came to Iowa State University, we purchased a modest older house that needed considerable fixing up. Every Saturday morning, I would compile my list of materials and tools needed to accomplish the weekend jobs and head for the local hardware store. There were usually three or four people working in the hardware department, but there was always a line waiting to talk to a young man who was quite personable and seemed to know everything there was to know about handling home improvement projects. He could immediately diagnose your problem, tell you what tool you needed, recommend what material you needed and describe the procedure for completing the job. Needless to say, he was a great asest to the hardware store.

Most local nurseries can help customers choose the proper plants and trees for their homes. By assisting the customer in understanding the growth patterns of trees and their degree of hardiness, these local stores can make many sales. They can also help customers diagnose plant diseases and problems with cultural practices. These are valuable services for consumers. Nurseries can also gain a lot of business by offering installation; that is, to plant trees and shrubs that customers purchase there. Most nurseries then guarantee these items for the first year and replace them if they should die. This is a powerful incentive for people who are short on time or who have never quite got the hang of planting certain types of plants.

Local consumer electronics stores usually offer extremely useful advice on the technical aspects of the equipment they sell. For example, they can decipher all the technical jargon that has evolved with respect to computers. In addition they can demonstrate the capabilities of the equipment and let the customer try his or her hand at it. Outside of the "category killer" type stores, very little expertise of this nature exists in most mass merchandise stores. As an example, I have purchased nearly all my computer equipment from our local computer store because of their oustanding service and repair facility. It has paid off on several occasions when, in the middle of an important project, the computer locks up or bombs out. When this happens, they are usually able to repair the machine the same day, which has been a lifesaver. In contrast, I have friends who have purchased computers by mail order. When they have trouble, some have had to send the computer to a repair facility in another part of the country and sometimes they don't get it back for three or four weeks. This would be an untenable situation for many people. Local stores should emphasize their service capabilities as a competitive advantage in every advertisement.

Most sporting goods equipment makers claim to have various unique and essential features that are little understood by the neophyte consumer. Again, most local sporting goods store personnel can explain these features and can assist the consumers in making the best decisions for themselves. Some sporting goods stores offer demonstrator equipment that customers can take on a "trial run" to see if it is really what they want. This type of service is just not available in the mass merchandise stores.

Advertise Your Technical Expertise

Local merchants can reinforce the image that they are the experts in their fields by writing newsletters and periodical articles for local newspapers, or by appearing on local radio and T.V. shows to discuss the pertinent issues of the day regarding their trade. For example, people all across the country are hungry for information regarding the care and maintenance of their lawns and gardens. Local lawn and garden personnel who dispense information in this manner will likely attract a lot of customers on the basis that they are dealing with real experts who can provide additional information when needed.

The mass merchandisers are not sitting still in this matter, however, Kmart has sponsored Jerry Baker on a call-in radio show for some time and sponsors his appearances at lawn and garden shows where he answers consumer questions. Wal-Mart has recently purchased the rights to use the *Better Homes and Gardens* name from the Meredeth Corporation. As part of the deal, Meredeth stipulated that Wal-Mart lawn and garden personnel must pass a test on the basics of horticulture before they can wear the *Better Homes and Gardens* logo on their uniform. As stated previously, Wal-Mart is experimenting with electronic kiosks where product selections can be made on the basis of input from the customer. In addition, Wal-Mart is marketing certain private label items under the *Better Homes and Gardens* logo. How can you effectively offer and advertise your expertise?

The Downside of Giving Advice

Examples of the expert technical advice available at local stores—and its importance to consumers—could go on and on, because it is a powerful competitive advantage for smaller stores, and in most cases probably could be developed even further. However, there are some downsides to dispensing this valuable information. Several fishing tackle dealers expressed the same dilemma. They explained that people who are in the market for a fish finder or depth finder will come into their stores and "pick their brains" about all the technical details of these machines. Once they acquire the information needed to make their selection, many then go down the street to a discount store and purchase it. Many times the purchaser would get the fish finder home and could not operate it in the manner expected. According to the dealers, many of these people then had the audacity to come back to their stores and again seek information on how to operate the machine.

Of course it is infuriating to local dealers when they are "used" as described above. Many are tempted to be rude, and in fact, a few actually are rude to the person and refuse to give information on something they did not sell. I highly encourage local merchants to "bite their lip" and "hold their tongue" in such a situation and try to be as nice to the person as possible. If merchants can view the situation as an educational opportunity and help the potential customer solve his or her problem, they can sell complementary merchandise, and attract some as full time customers. Not all of these people will become regular customers, but a merchant is better off getting a few new customers in this manner than losing them all, which almost certainly would happen if they were rude and refused to help.

A personal experience illustrates how one customer (me) reacted to a similar situation. Several years ago, I purchased one of the early mulching lawn mowers from a local dealer. It was a name brand mower, but in my opinion had some design flaws and never worked very well. It definitely was under-powered, and the mower deck and the blade seemed to be poorly designed. The mower continually choked up and would "kill" the engine, after which it would not re-start until it had cooled for 15 to 20 minutes. I took the mower back to the dealer several times and he and I worked in good faith, trying whatever either of us thought might help solve the problems. Nothing we tried seemed to help. After a couple of years, I spotted another brand of mulching mower at a new dealership in town. It seemed to me to be much better designed so I traded in my old mower for the new model. The new mower worked quite well and I got along very well with it the first year. The next spring when I took it in for its annual checkup, I found the new dealer had just gone out of business.

Without thinking, I took the mower to my original dealer thinking he would appreciate the business and the $35 he would earn from changing the plug, sharpening the blade and cleaning the air filter. Instead I was met with a barrage of swear words and derisive comments. Among other things included in this tirade, he told me I was stupid for buying an inferior brand from an unreliable dealer. He further stated that he had no responsibility for servicing my mower and that he did not want to see me in his place of business again. He did not have to tell me twice. I left immediately and have not been back since. For the next few years, I performed my own maintenance. I have since bought a new lawn mower and a new snow blower, but I did not buy from this inhospitable dealer.

Some local merchants are much more cunning in dealing with customers who have bypassed them and purchased something at a mass merchant's store. The owner of a lawn equipment store told me how he deals with the problem. He said that when someone brings in a mower that was purchased at a discount store and complains about something not working right he uses the following procedure. Although he usually knows full well what the problem is, he will call his mechanic over and the conversation goes like this: "Joe, this gentleman bought this lawn mower down at Sav Mart and it's backfiring through the air cleaner." Joe then responds with, "Well, that's a new one on me, we've never seen that problem before; I wouldn't know where to start to fix that." The owner then tells the gentleman, "That sounds pretty serious to me, I believe you should take it back to Sav Mart and ask for a new one."

Note that in the above example, the owner of the lawn equipment store and his mechanic were not rude to the potential customer, but they shunted him aside in a deceitful way, and probably had a big laugh when he left. It's one way of doing business, but a better way to handle this situation is to offer to fix the mower for a fee. This would provide a little income and might very well impress the customer to the point that he will buy his next mower from the lawn equipment store.

OFFER DELIVERY AND/OR PICK-UP SERVICE WHERE APPROPRIATE

Offering delivery and/or pick-up service often will enable a merchant to capture a share of the market that might otherwise escape. Many years ago it was common to have milk and groceries delivered, as well as a host of other things. It was also common to have your laundry and dry cleaning picked up, as well as as your appliances and autos that could better be repaired in the shop. As our economy moved more and more to a self service mode, many of these services were abandoned. In many ways we have come full circle and again have a need for such services. Many people simply do not have the time or the transportation to accomplish these things for themselves.

Some druggists have found that by offering free delivery of prescriptions and other items, they can attract a certain segment of the market, in particular, shut-ins, elderly, and single parents, as well as just plain busy people.

Hardware dealers have found that by delivering heavy or bulky items such as riding lawn mowers, ladders, and building materials they can carve out a certain share of the consumer market. Some hardware stores also offer prompt delivery of building materials to builders and contractors as a way of meeting their needs and getting their business.

Lawn and garden stores and nurseries can make a lot of sales by offering delivery service. Bulky items and heavy items such as trees, bales of mulch, patio blocks, and landscape timers are difficult for most consumers to transport. In such cases, the delivery service can be the deciding factor in making the sale.

Owners of major appliance stores and consumer electronics stores have also found pick-ups and deliveries to be an effective tool in attracting customers and making sales. Many customers simply do not have the capability to move heavy appliances around on their own and they gravitate to stores which offer this service.

Several years ago the refrigerator in our rental house quit on a Friday afternoon after a three day Fourth of July weekend. I quickly went to a mass merchandise store which handled major appliances. I spotted the refrigerator I wanted to buy, but was informed by the salesperson that it would be some time next week before they could deliver it to my rental property. I quickly drove to another discount store and again was informed that it would be at least a week before the refrigerator could be delivered. Finally I went to my local appliance store and found an appropriate replacement refrigerator. Upon hearing my dilemma, the owner said, "if you buy the refrigerator now, I will have it at your house within an hour." I bought, he delivered, and I have been a steady customer there ever since.

I have heard many similar stores in my travels about local merchants who have secured loyal customers by being alert to meeting their needs with respect to delivery and/or pick up. Even though local merchants can offer personal and efficient delivery service, they need to be aware that some of the mass merchants such as Home Depot, Home Quarters, Builder's Square and others have also caught on to the importance of delivery and offer it at an extra cost. If you are offering free delivery, then advertise that fact on a regular basis.

OFFER CLINICS, WORKSHOPS, AND CLASSES

There are millions of people who would like to be "do-it-yourselfers" but they simply do not have the knowledge or training to accomplish the job. Many merchants have figured out ways to offer clinics, workships and classes to educate customers to accomplish common household tasks which they might otherwise hire out to get done.

My first encounter with such a workshop was shortly after I came to Iowa State University. Our "fixer-upper" house needed quite a bit of work, including some wallpapering. I had never papered a wall in my life, but I noticed that one of our local stores was sponsoring a two night wall papering workshop. I attended the classes and found that even though I cannot do many home maintenance jobs well, I could wallpaper pretty well. I papered that house and later papered all of our new home built the next year. I really appreciated the fact that the store had taught me a new skill that I enjoyed and that saved me a lot of money. In repayment, I have become a loyal customer to this wallpaper and paint store and shop there to this day.

These types of classes can be effective for many types of stores, including lawn and garden stores which can teach basic pruning, disease identification, insect identification, etc. Camera stores can teach the basics of photography can make additional sales. Fabric stores can offer sewing classes to capture additional trade. Fishing tackle dealers who offer clinics on the basics of different types of fishing attract new customers. Gun dealers who offer hunting clinics also attract new clientele.

Again, some of the mass merchandisers such as Home Depot understand the importance of offering these types of training sessions and schedule them free to consumers on a regular basis. A word of caution is offered here. Extreme care should be used when offering classes on certain subjects particularly where city codes require licensed personnel to install electrical or plumbing fixtures, or if there is a chance that class members could be physically injured as a result of alleged inadequate instruction.

OFFER OTHER SERVICES

Customers are continually seeking out more services, and stores which offer them not only attract customers for the services, but usually make additional complementary sales of merchandise. Several hardware dealers have worked with employees to compile lists of services performed in the store. Most hardware store personnel are astounded at the sheer number of services that they offer. Even more importantly, customers are very impressed when they see the new lists of services posted around the store. Even regular customers are not aware of some of the services available. You cannot sell services if customers do not know about them. The following list is one that was compiled by an outstanding hardware dealer.

Services Available

- Ceramic tile cutting
- Chain cutting

- Computer color matching
- Free delivery (on purchases over $150)
- Glass cutting
- Handle installation (rakes, shovels, axes, etc.)
- Kerosene service
- Key duplicating
- Lawn mower repair and service
- Lock re-keying
- LP gas service
- Lumber cutting
- Paint mixing
- Post office
- Rope cutting
- Screen cutting
- Screen repair
- Sharpening service (knives, saws, scissors, mower blades, etc.)
- Special order catalog (over 50,000 items)
- Sprinkler system design
- Tool rentals
- Window repair
- Window shade cutting

This is an impressive list of services for a hardware store to offer. This store operator placed a large sign listing the services at the entry to the store. In addition he placed smaller adhesive-backed lists at strategic places around the store. He and other hardware owners who have compiled and displayed the lists insist that sales increase because of them.

Some drug stores also have developed service centers as a way of attracting additional customers to the store. One drug store chain in particular has made arrangements to host a branch post office. In addition, they offer the following services:

- Free blood pressure testing service
- Facilities for sending express mail
- Facsimile sending and receiving
- Packaging and mailing
- Copying machines

- Sign making machines
- Business card printing
- Computer rental (in-store)
- Rental of home health care items

There is little question that providing a one-stop service center has helped the overall sales of these drug stores.

Lawn and garden stores have recognized the importance of services as well, including the following:

- Soil testing
- Plant disease diagnosis
- Insect identification
- Free liquid fertilizer
- Free delivery of bulky items such as trees, bales of mulch, concrete blocks, etc.
- Re-potting of plants
- Tool sharpening services
- Tool rental
- Landscape planning service

Lawn and garden centers which offer services such as these tend to be much more succesful than those that don't.

ENSURE A SPEEDY CHECKOUT

In this era of fast food, overnight delivery and facsimile machines, customers are accustomed to speedy service and expect to get through the checkout line quickly. When they have to wait more than a few minutes they become very upset. The mass merchandisers know this and have adopted high technology devices (such as scanners) to speed customers through the checkout line. Most mass merchandisers also have cross trained their stockers to fill in as checkout cashiers when needed. Wal-Mart, for example, has signs in every checkout lane stating that if more than three people are waiting in line they will open other checkout lines.

Many local merchants have not adopted high technology checkout equipment. In spite of that, some of the better merchants still manage to get customers through the checkout line in a hurry by having plenty of personnel around. However, many lcoal merchants have antiquated methods of checking out customers. For example some have a system where they have to hand write a sales receipt for each sale—usually a slow process. Sometimes the price is not tagged on the item and this causes delays while various means are used to track it down. Sometimes the cash register does not automatically compute the sales tax so calculators, tax tables or hand calculations must be used. All of these processes slow down the checkout process.

A couple of years ago I worked with a major hardware chain and spoke at two of their shows. One of the things I was asked to emphasize was the adoption of modern technology in the form of computers and scanner checkout. Attendees were asked to submit questions after the seminar that I would answer and then the answers would be disseminated via a periodical newsletter. I was amazed that I had several similar comments indicating a refusal to adopt modern technology. Most of the respondents claimed that they had an "old fashioned" hardware store which they prized. They made it clear that adopting new technology would ruin their stores since it would destory the old fashioned image. They may have had a point, but I still believe that most of today's shoppers would prefer a quick modern checkout to a slow old fashioned checkout.

ACCEPT CREDIT CARDS

Most local merchants accept credit cards of various types, primarily the bank cards. However, there are some who still believe that this is an unnecessary cost of doing business. After a recent seminar, the owner of a bookstore located in the local shopping mall came forward and asked me if I thought he should accept credit cards in his book store. He said customers regularly ask if he accepts credit cards. I asked if he was losing sales because of not accepting credit cards. He said, "perhaps, some, but I just can't see giving up all that money to the credit card companies for handling the purchase." At that time a couple who owned a local sporting goods store had overheard the conversation and, before I could respond, they emphaticlaly stated in unison, "Do it!" The couple said that they too had resisted credit cards in their business, but gradually realized that they were losing sales in cases where customers spotted something they wanted but did not have enough cash on them or did not have enough balance in their checking account to pay for the purchase. They said that they made arrangements to accept bank cards at a 2–1/2 percent fee to the bank. They claimed that it increased their sales substantially and cut down on their bad check frequency. The couple sold the book store owner on the benefits of accepting credit cards. Obviously the rates paid to credit card companies by the merchants will vary, so it pays to shop around.

Buying merchandise with credit cards has become a way of life for many people and they pass up purchases and shun stores that do not accept them. In other words, many consumers now consider the acceptance of credit cards a necessary service. It is in the best interest of most stores to accept credit cards. This is especially true if a good share of your customers are from out of town or if you get a lot of transient traffic, because use of a credit card eliminates the chance of getting a bad check.

QUALITY COMMITMENT STEPS TO BETTER CUSTOMER SERVICE

Smaller stores can gain great competitive advantage in offering more specialized and better service than most of the mass merchandisers. Owners and managers of local stores need to make a strong commitment to service or they may find that customers perceive that they are no better than the mass merchandisers. Therefore, management must set the tone and see to it that employees are trained as well as possible as possible to carry out the tradition of outstanding service.

1. **Make sure that your employees are knowledgeable.** Employees should know as much as possible about the products they sell and should be fully aware of company policies and procedures. It may be a good idea to team them with experierenced employees so they can learn by asking and observing. They should be selected to attend any company schools available. Employees should also be asked to keep a notebook of questions or situations they could not handle, with the express purpose of finding the answers as soon as possible.

2. **Determine if there is a demand for deliveries or pick-ups.** If it is obvious that deliveries or pickups could increase your business, by all means, implement them if you can. Delivery vehicles and personnel should be the most economical for the job. In the case of pharmaceuticals, food, and flowers a small economical vehicle and perhaps an entry level employee are sufficient. If you plan to deliver heavier items such as building supplies, furniture, farm supplies, it may be necessary to have specialized, heavier duty vehicles and more experienced employees to make deliveries or pickups.

   A decision must be made regarding whether a fee will be charged or whether the services will be free. Some businesses choose to charge for all deliveries or pickups. Others offer free delivery. Still others charge for longer distances or for small purchases, but offer free services within a shorter radius or for purchases over a certain amount. Many customers do not mind paying an extra charge if they feel that the product or service is priced reasonably. Free deliveries or pickups are best, wherever possible, with the additional costs built in to the prices. In either case, there should be no surprises for the customer. There is nothing worse for a store's image than delivering an item to a customer and then asking for a delivery fee when they thought the service was free. A misunderstanding can be avoided by placing prominent signs in strategic areas of the store, stating the delivery policy. It should also be reiterated at the time of the sale.

3. **Make a commitment to offering classes, workshops or clinics for your customers.** If you feel that there is a need by current or prospective customers to learn certain skills in order to use more of your products, offer them. The presenters should be knowledgeable and could include store personnel, company representatives, or other experts such as extension agents, community college teachers or high school vocational teachers. The classes should preferably be free, but most customers would pay a nominal fee for good instruction. The classes should be well taught, with hands on experience using store products. This is also the ideal time to offer class participants special values for certain merchandise to get them going on their own.

4. **Offer other services that will attract customers.** Today's customers do not enjoy running all over town to take care of life's daily chores. Determine if by offering other services you could attract additional customers while helping them to save time. This may mean re-setting your store in order to make room. This would be a good time to weed out slow moving merchandise and use the space to accommodate the new services. When new services are incorporated, customers should be advised through advertising and in-store signs. Usage of the services should be monitored to determine if they are popular with customers and generate increased traffic. Some experimentation may be necessary to find the mix of services that generate the maximum traffic. Sales of regular store products or services should also be monitored to find if the additional traffic is generating additional sales. If not, perhaps repositioning impulse items near the services area may assist in this regard.

5. **Ensure that customers are being checked out in a speedy and efficient manner.** If your cash registers are obsolete, consider getting new ones that are connected to scanners. Technology has improved; in recent years prices have decreased and many small businesses can now afford this

type of equipment. When properly set up, inventory control and accounting can be improved immeasurably.

6. **Accept credit cards.** At least try accepting credit cards on a trial basis if you are skeptical about its effect on your business. Customers have come to expect credit card acceptance and will pass up any businesses that do not accept them.

7

TREATING THE CUSTOMER RIGHT

Customer relations refers to the manner in which customers are treated while doing business with a firm, whether it be in the store, on the phone, in the home or in other settings. Studies have repeatedly shown that the primary reason that customers quit doing business with a firm and never come back is because they feel that they have been mistreated in some way. This perceived mistreatment can take many forms such as shoddy workmanship, failure to have items ready when promised, failure to deliver items or perform service when scheduled, a bad experience with a returned item, being treated rudely by a store employee or owner, etc.

Practically everyone has a personal list of horror stories of various mistreatments suffered when dealing with retail stores. When this subject comes up in social or business groups, nearly every story ends with the story teller stating, "and that is the last time I will ever go in there."

A recent experience of friends offers a telling example of what many people endure. The carpet in their family room needed to be replaced. After weeks of comparing various carpet samples, they finally settled on a beautiful green carpet from a local carpet store chain. Unfortunately, the carpet they wanted was not in stock, but they were assured that the carpet would be installed in plenty of time for a reception they had been planning for some of their colleagues at work. The carpet took longer to arrive than they had been told and was pushing the date when they wanted it installed. Finally, they were called and told that the installer would be at their house on Thursday morning at 9:00 a.m. to install the new carpet. The wife stayed home from work to let the installer in and supervise the job. At 11:00 a.m. she called and asked her husband if he could come home and wait for the installer, since she had an appointment at work. The husband juggled his schedule and went home because the installer was supposed to arrive "at any minute." After lunch, he called and was told that the installer would now arrive at 2:00 p.m. To make a long story short, several promises were made to get the installer right over throughout Thursday and Friday, but he never showed. On Saturday morning our friends called and "read the riot act" to the salesman. He said they normally did not install on Saturday, but in this case he would get an installer out to do the job. Again after several calls (always initiated by our friends) and no action they finally gave up. At 8:30 p.m. on Saturday night the door bell rang and a young man announced that he was there to install the carpet. The husband said it was too late, but his wife decided that they had better take it while they could. After listening to the flip remarks of the installer for a few minutes, the husband decided he had better leave for awhile before he blew his top. When he came back about an hour later, a roll of ugly gray carpet lay on the family room floor. The wrong carpet had been ordered! At that point our friends cancelled the order.

The next day they ordered a similar carpet from an independent store. It came in on time, the installer arrived at precisely the time designated and the carpet was laid in a quick and professional manner. After a few days, the saleslady called to make sure that our friends were satisfied with the carpet and the installation. That is quite a contrast in how two similar firms do business and you can guess which one our friends will buy their carpet from in the future.

THE IMPORTANCE OF GOOD CUSTOMER RELATIONS

Many merchants treat the subject of customer relations as "a problem for other merchants, but of little importance for my business." In other words, they do not perceive that they have many problems with customer dissatisfaction. Nearly all businesses end up with at least some unhappy customers, but the problem is that many do not complain to the company where the problem occurred.

Figure 7.1 shows the results of studies done by Technical Assistance Research Programs, Inc. (TARP), a Washington, D.C. based research firm that has conducted studies for the White House, the National Science Foundation and a number of private companies. These studies indicate that 60% of dissatisfied customers do not complain when they have a problem with a business that sells large ticket durable goods. Fifty percent of customers having problems with companies that sell medium ticket items do not complain when they have a problem. Customers seem to complain most when they are dealing with suppliers of large ticket services (e.g., auto repair, home repair, etc.). Even these types of businesses have 37% of their customers who are non-complainers.

The deceiving thing about these non-complainers is that even though they are not complaining to the business they are mad at, they certainly are not reticent about telling other people about their problems. An earlier TARP study found that, on average, a customer who has had an unpleasant experience with a business, will tell 9 or 10 other people. The study found that in 13% of the cases, the customers told 20 or more people about the bad experience. Usually these "horror stories" get embellished and exaggerated with each telling. This can only be bad news for the business, since it almost certainly drives away at least some potential customers, if not some current ones.

Figure 7-1 Many Customers Do Not Complain
(Percentage of Customers Experiencing Problems With Selected Products/Services Who Did Not Complain)

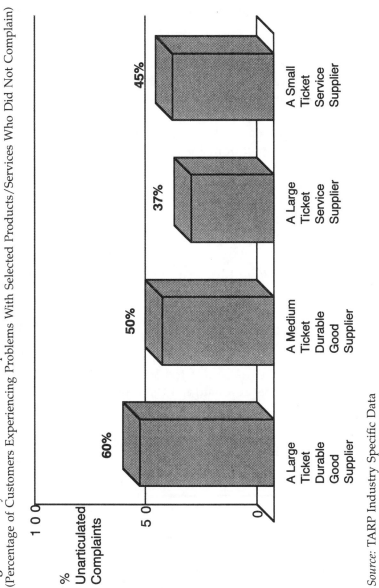

Source: TARP Industry Specific Data

Why don't customers come back to the business and complain more often? The TARP studies found responses such as:

- "It's not worth my time or trouble."
- "Complaining will do no good—no one cares."
- "I don't know where or how to complain."

Some of us are also intimidated by owners and managers; we dread the big confrontation. In other cases, we like the business person and are afraid of hurting his or her feelings by telling some of the outrageous things that happen to us. Most customers are not proud of the fact that they aren't "leveling" with business owners or managers when they have problems. It's just that we have had so many bad experiences when we tried to complain in the past, that we genuinely believe it is not worth our time or effort. Figure 7-2 illustrates this point quite well by showing that as many as 74% of customers did not get an acceptable response when they offered a complaint to a business.

The TARP studies showed that if you can get customers to come in and complain when they have a problem, considerably more can be turned into repeat customers, compared to the non-complainers. This is illustrated in Figure 7-3. As can be seen from the chart, the biggest share of the unhappy customers can be turned into repeat customers when the complaint is resolved quickly. The logical conclusion from these studies is to encourage customers to complain to store personnel when they are unhappy about something. Figure 7-4 shows the huge return on investment when special efforts are made to handle complaints efficiently.

HOW TO HANDLE COMPLAINTS

It is obvious that it is in the best interests of businesses to solicit complaints. The question is how can it be done in an effective manner. The TARP report suggested the following steps.

1. Solicit complaints—make it easy for unhappy customers to tell you about their problems.

Figure 7-2 Many Customers Are Not Happy With Business' Response To Their Complaints
(Percentage of Complaintants Reporting a Less Than Acceptable Response to Their Consumer Problem)

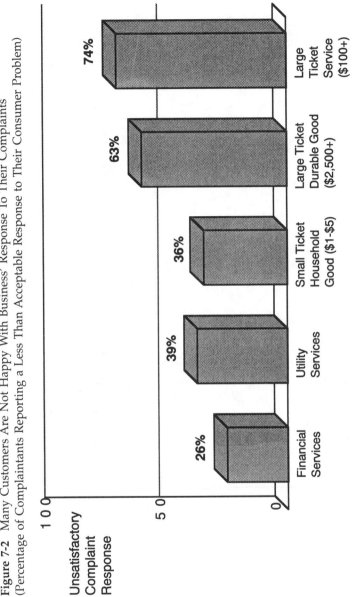

Unsatisfactory Complaint Response

100

50

0

26% Financial Services

39% Utility Services

36% Small Ticket Household Good ($1-$5)

63% Large Ticket Durable Good ($2,500+)

74% Large Ticket Service ($100+)

Source: TARP Industry Specific Data

Figure 7-3 How Many Of Your Unhappy Customers Will Buy From You Again?

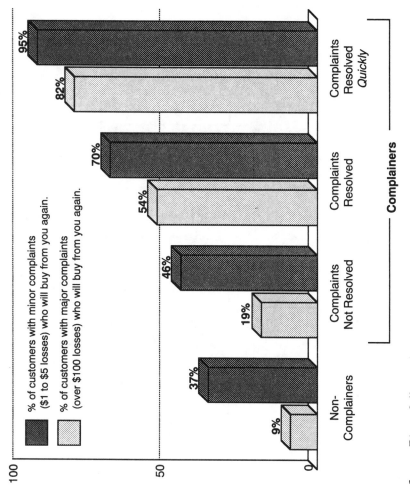

Source: Direct Selling Education Foundation

Figure 7-4 Return on Investment By Corporate Complaint Handling Units

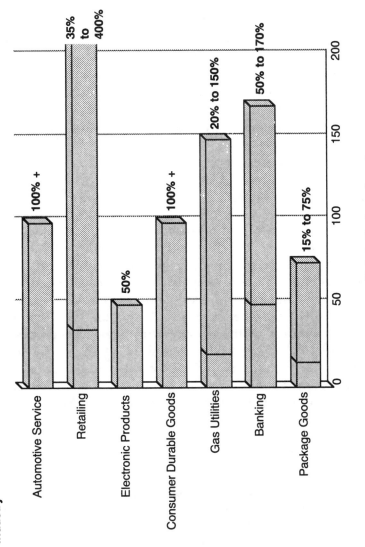

Source: TARP Industry Specific Data

2. Solve customer complaints as quickly as possible and with a smile.

3. Keep records of why complaints occur.

4. Analyze how complaints can be prevented and make changes in your products and marketing procedures when appropriate.

5. Provide incentives to encourage your employees to carry out the policies described above.

Soliciting Complaints

Customers should be encouraged in every way possible to let your business know when they are unhappy about something. It can begin with signs in the store. A good place for signs is at the checkout counters. To be most effective, they should be at about eye level for the average person. They should invite the customer to tell store personnel when they have a problem. It is also a good idea to place some type of motto on shopping bags such as "We're not happy until you are happy, please tell us if you have a problem." Similar mottos could be placed on receipts and statements.

Some companies even advertise to solicit complaints. Newspaper advertisements have stated, "We know we're not perfect. If you have a problem, please let us know, we want to take care of it." Similar versions of this have been used in the broadcast media.

When customers see these invitations over and over, they will become more inclined to share their problems with you. However, your company must be completely prepared to handle the complaints in a timely and satisfactory manner or your advertising dollars will have been spent in vain. In fact, the backlash from mishandling customer complaints could do your company more harm than the original event that caused the unhappiness.

Solve the Customer Complaints as Quickly as Possible

Before a campaign of complaint solicitation is begun, everyone in the business must be told about it, and apprised of its rationale and its importance. Furthermore, they should be trained on their duties and responsibilities in the process. Employees who have customer contact should be empowered or authorized to solve the customer's problems in all but the most unusual circumstances.

Some of the mass merchandisers do an outstanding job of empowering employees to handle problems. For example, Wal-Mart has a policy of meeting any competitor's advertised price. One night I was about to depart for our local grocery store which is located along side our Wal-Mart store. My son asked if I would purchase an over-the-counter skin medication for him. I went to the grocery store first and did my shopping. As I went by the skin medication, I made a mental note of the price, because I assumed that it would be lower priced at Wal-Mart and I would buy it there. When I got to the Wal-Mart store, I found the skin medication was 15 cents higher at Wal-Mart than at the grocery store. Nevertheless, I took it to the checkout counter, but I mentioned to the cashier that the item was 15 cents less at the grocery store. She rang up the sale at the supermarket price, even though this was outside the range of their offer. Kmart and Target have similar policies.

Target stores have a policy that if a price is not marked on an item or if it is not bar coded, they will take the customer's word on the price (within reason). This saves the hassle of calling over the public address system for someone back in the department to do a price check. More importantly, it eliminates the hassle for customers and speeds them through the checkout line.

Keep Records of Why Complaints Occur

Store personnel should list the various complaints they receive on a daily basis. The real objective of a retail owner/manager is to eliminate the source of the complaint so that it does not happen again. Records of complaint are invaluable in accomplishing this goal. Many complaints may be random happenings, for example, a defective product, an unavoidable delay in meeting a schedule, etc. However, when the records start showing a pattern of complaints, such as a high percentage of customers complaining of the checkout being too slow, or expressing dissatisfaction with the returns policy, then it is time to take action to eliminate the source of the problem.

Analyze Complaints and Take Action to Prevent Recurrence

Keeping records of complaints will accomplish little, unless they are analyzed to determine the root causes. Once the causes are determined, then corrective action can be taken. For example, the carpet salesman who promised delivery dates and times that were never met did not have access to the carpet layers' schedules. If a master schedule had been kept current for all carpet layers, salespeople should have been able to schedule on-time installations.

If a certain product has a high return rate because of defects, the supplier should be notified immediately. If defect-free replacements cannot be delivered quickly, then the merchant might want to change brands or change suppliers.

Here's another example of how a simple offense can affect sales. In one of our focus group studies, we found that the majority of customers for a women's clothing store were offended by the owner smoking a cigar continually throughout the day and by various employees smoking cigarettes in the store. They did not like breathing the secondary smoke, but their main complaint was that the smoke smell permeated the fabric of the garments. Of course, the solution to this problem was for the owner and employees to go outside to smoke. Sales picked up considerably once word got around that the store was smoke-free.

Provide Incentives to Employees

Employees should constantly be encouraged to perform in a quality manner. They should be praised when handling customer complaints single-handedly. They should not be penalized when handling a customer problem in a different manner than the owner/manager would like. As time goes on, more and more companies will offer profit sharing to employees. Giving employees a share of the profit provides the ultimate incentive for working together as a team to identify customer problems and solving them.

PRACTICING THE GOLDEN RULE

Finding out about customer complaints and solving them is very important, but even more important is running the business so that the *number of complaints is minimized.* A lot of this comes down to treating customers just as we would like to be treated. The following practices can help in keeping customers happy.

Greet and/or Acknowledge All Customers

Studies have shown that the thing that bothers customers more than anything else is *being ignored when they are in the store.* This includes not being greeted when entering the store, being ignored when a salesperson is with another customer, being ignored when a salesperson is on a telephone call, etc.

Stores should be set up so that customers entering the store will have immediate contact with store personnel. As big as Wal-Mart stores are, they have solved this problem by stationing a greeter at the entrance to greet and assist every person entering the store. In many stores, customers must diligently search for a store representative, sometimes to no avail. Once while inspecting a regional discount store in upstate New York, I was asked by five customers within five minutes, "Sir, can you tell me where to find the towels," "Sir, can you tell me the price on this item," and other such questions. Apparently, customers assumed that I worked for the store because I was wearing a suit and tie. As I looked around, I could not identify any store personnel.

This brings up another good point. Good stores provide some distinctive identification for store personnel. In some cases it might be a smock of a certain color, tee shirts of a certain color or perhaps a distinctive badge or name tag. The main point in this is to help the customer identify store personnel easily and quickly.

A very common occurrence in many stores is that during busy times, sales personnel get involved with a customer and they ignore all new customers until they finish business with the current customer. A better solution to this problem is for the salesperson to excuse herself or himself momentarily from the current customer, to make eye contact with the new customer and in a very friendly manner, say, "Good morning sir, I'll be with you in about five minutes." Most customers will accept this, but they won't accept being ignored.

Likewise, on many occasions store representatives on the telephone will turn their back to the customer so that they do not have to deal with them until they are finished on the telephone. This is particularly insulting when the person is obviously involved in a personal call. Again, the preferred method of handling this situation, is to excuse oneself from the business caller momentarily, turn to the new customer and again, making eye contact, tell the person, "I will be with you in about two minutes." When the call is of a personal nature, the solution is to terminate the call immediately and deal with the new customer.

Another thing that infuriates customers is to wait while store personnel complete paperwork before assisting the customer. One night I flew into a North Carolina airport, arriving about 10:00 p.m., about two hours behind schedule. I had a prior reservation for a rental car from a major car rental company and I still had about two hours to drive to get to my destination. I approached the counter where the attendant was sorting through some invoices. I was the only customer there, but she was so involved in her invoice work that she did not look up to acknowledge my presence. I cleared my throat loudly to get her attention, to no avail. After another 15 or 20 seconds, I plopped by credit card and drivers license on the counter as loudly as I could, but nothing could deter her from her important invoice business. Finally after being ignored for about a minute, I said in a loud and not too friendly voice, "I think I have a reservation." Finally, the woman looked up in a very perturbed manner and grudgingly took care of my car rental. In the attendant's mind, I'm sure that she felt the invoices were the most important item of the moment, whereas in may mind I felt that getting the rental car and getting on with my trip was the most important event of the moment. Who was right? As the old cliche goes, *the customer is always right,* and I would add, should have first priority. If a company has its paperwork in perfect order, but ignores its customers, it soon will have no paperwork to do other than bankruptcy procedures. The car rental company obviously had not properly trained this clerk.

Perhaps the most frustrating thing that customers encounter is being ignored when they genuinely want to purchase something in a store. When friends built a new house several years ago, they needed a special bench to fit under the breakfast counter. They finally found the perfect bench in a large Des Moines furniture store. However, at the time they were squeezed for money so they temporarily postponed the purchase. A few months later they had the money in their bank account and the husband had to make a trip through Des Moines. On a Monday morning at 10:00 a.m. he drove up to the store in his van. He entered the store and walked directly back to the bench and was ready to buy. He even took out his checkbook and was ready to write the check for $300 plus. But no one would pay any attention to him. There were few customers in the store and there were store personnel running in every direction. Finally, he touched a sales lady on the arm as she was rushing by and said "I want to buy this bench." Her response was, "I'm sorry sir, I can't help you, I'm taking inventory, go talk to the manager over there." He walked over to the manager's counter, but he was deeply engrossed in discussing last weekend's golf game with two friends and my friend could not get his attention. He left the store and has never been back. A good store manager would have set the example of always putting customers first and he would have given employees authority to interrupt tasks involving things to take care of matters involving customers.

Shortly thereafter, my friend found a woodworker at a crafts fair who was showing furniture much like he was seeking. The craftsman came to their house, took measurements, sketched out a design and custom built a better quality bench than they had planned to buy and at less cost. They have ordered several more pieces of furniture from this craftsman over the years.

The old analogy of treating customers like one would treat guests in one's home has a lot of validity. Certainly a good host would not continue working on the family budget when a friend came to visit. Nor would a host tell a guest, "I cannot visit with you I have to clean out the sock drawers." Such hosts would not have friends for long after such treatment. Merchants need to keep the same principles in mind; treat the customers as well or better than if they were guests in our homes. The smaller local merchant who offers truly responsive customer service will easily stand out from the rest.

Offer a Smile in Every Aisle

This expression may seem trite, but there is little doubt that the vast majority of customers prefer to do business in a store where they are treated in a friendly manner as contrasted to an unfriendly or indifferent manner. A very successful grocery chain headquartered in Iowa feels so strongly about this that they adopted the motto of "a helpful smile in every aisle." They conclude their television commercials with a jingle about a helpful smile in every aisle, featuring various employees smiling at the camera. This type of advertising has at least three positive effects.

1. It appeals to customers.
2. It is a great way to give recognition to employees.
3. It sends a strong message to employees that this is standard operating procedure.

Customers' perception of how friendly a store is usually can be traced back to how the owner/manager treats customers and employees. Employees tend to follow the example set by the boss. Several years ago, I was visiting with the owner of a local household appliance store. We were standing just outside of the rear of the store when one of his delivery vehicles drove up with a new washer and dryer strapped in the rear. Following along in a car was the intended customer. As the truck stopped the owner yelled at the driver, "what are you doing back here?" The driver said the customer refused to accept the washer and dryer. By that time the customer had exited his car and said, "That dryer has a dent in it, I want one without a dent." The owner, in turn yelled, "What is the matter with you, that little dent won't hurt anything." He then told the driver "I'm not giving him another dryer, take that one back to his house." Upon which the customer said, "I refuse to accept the dryer in that condition, cancel the order and give me money back!" After much ado, the owner sent him to the cashier to get his money and warned him never to set foot in his store again. He needn't have told the customer, because I'm sure that wild horses could not have dragged him back into the store again. You would not have to be clairvoyant to see that this store would not stay in business long. In fact, it went out of business less than a year after this incident.

How could an owner such as the one described above ever expect a smile in every aisle from his employees when he was setting the worst possible example himself? Wal-Mart officials used to feel so strongly about this matter that they required their new associates to wear a smiley button that said, "If I fail to smile, you get this." Pinned to the bottom of the badge was a new dollar bill. More than one associate has lost his or her dollar bill when customers accused them of not smiling. I have not seen this for a few years in Wal-Mart stores, I suspect because they came to realize that the practice was somewhat demeaning to associates. However, there is little doubt that the practice sent a strong message to both the associates and to customers that the company was serious about treating customers in a friendly manner.

Owners and managers of local stores need to begin by setting the example, and should create some incentives for their employees to vigorously participate. Some stores have an ongoing Friendliest Employee Contest where every month customers are asked to make comments on the friendliness of employees. In some stores a photo is prominently displayed indicating the winner. In others, winners are given some type of monetary award such as a gift certificate to a nice restaurant, etc. Some chambers of commerce use secret shoppers to find the friendliest sales clerk in town, with the winner getting a nice award and a lot of recognition.

Learn How to Handle Irate Customers

Nearly every business encounters an irate customer at one time or another. How these people are handled can make a big difference in the success or failure of a business. Here again I reiterate the old saying that it takes months to get a new customer, but only seconds to lose one. I often ask audiences, "What is the worst thing you can do when an irate customer appears upon the scene?" In the peaceful confines of a conference room, most participants respond with such things as, "argue with them," "get irate back at them," "yell at them," etc. However, in the heat of battle, many store personnel cannot maintain that poise and common sense. Here's another example. A friend had taken his car to a local repair shop to have some malady fixed. When he went to pick up the car he found that the shop had replaced some dubious components without his permission, and the bill was about three times what he had expected. Upon inquiring of the owner as to why non-essential components had been replaced and why the bill was so high, a heated argument quickly ensued. At this time the owner of the shop grabbed a large "monkey wrench" and threatened to beat the customer over the head if he did not pay his bill and get out of there. This story, with embellishments, along with other stories of a similar nature made the rounds around town. As would be expected, this business also was closed within a year.

Owners can employ the LEAR method in handling irate customers. LEAR is merely an acronym for a four-step process. This process is not my original theory, but I cannot find the originator to give attribution. The four-step process is described below.

1. **Listen.** It is only human nature to become defensive when someone assaults you verbally in an aggressive manner. Many of us, however, start thinking ahead as to what our response is going to be. We become so engrossed in thinking how we are going to prove the customer wrong that we fail to listen to what the customer is saying. If we have to ask the customer to repeat something he or she just

said, their blood pressure may go up another 10 points. From the outset, store personnel should put aside everything else and give the customer their undivided attention. Let's face it, irate customers are not there for entertainment; they are there because they feel that something about their transaction with your store has gone wrong.

2. **Empathize.** Empathize means to put yourself in the shoes of the other person. How would you feel about the situation if the same thing happened to you? Your body language can help convey to the customer that you are concerned, so a few positive head nods and lots of eye contact can help calm the customer. Avoid the folded arm stance, because it can indicate defiance.

3. **Ask questions.** It is important to let customers get the anger out of their systems before beginning a dialog with them. Once they have calmed down, it is essential to begin a questioning process to make sure that all the facts are on the table. Sometimes customers are in such a state that they are irrational and often leave out or misstate certain facts. It is usually helpful to begin asking questions in a chronological order from the time the trouble began through the various stages to the present time.

4. **Resolve the problem.** It is essential that the problem be resolved. Merchants all across the country have told me that they have found the most effective method for resolving such problems is merely to ask the customer what she or he sees as a reasonable solution to the problem. I hear figures like nine times out of 10 customers are surprisingly reasonable in their demands. If the merchant then agrees to the solution, a win-win solution has occurred. The burden for a reasonable solution is put on the customer and when the merchant agrees to it there is little room for disappointment. Studies have found that if stores can get customers to come in and complain when they are unhappy about something, most will return to do business again, whereas

customers who do not complain usually just walk away and never come back.

Send the Customer Away in a Good Mood

Managing the customer's mood is no small task. Customers can have a good experience in a store until checkout time. Then they encounter a cashier who has had a bad day and takes it out on them. Cashiers may, with eyes downcast, slam the change on the counter and mumble something like, "I'll sure be glad when I get out of here and get a real job." This is an affront to the customer and sends her or him away with a sour taste in the mouth. This is quite a contrast to the stores that train their cashiers to make eye contact with the customer, and with a genuine smile thank them for shopping in the store, adding reassuring remarks such as "We have sold a lot of those items and customers are really happy with their performance." Sometimes customers have agonized over the purchase of a certain item, and they appreciate the reassurance that they have made a good decision. Management of the customer's experience starts when they walk in, and ends when they walk out.

DON'T PRE-JUDGE CUSTOMERS

Retail store personnel sometimes pre-judge customers as they enter the store on the basis of their dress, their manner of speech, or other personal characteristics. This can be a big mistake. A friend of mine told me a story about his daughter. She had graduated from college with a major in retailing. She quickly found a job with a leading department store in a Texas city, where she became the manager of the fine china and crystal department. One day she observed an incident involving a man who appeared to be a laborer, based on his soiled clothes and unkempt appearance. As he walked into the china and crystal department, one of the young sales clerks approached him and asked if he needed help. He said, "No thanks, I'm just looking." Upon which the sales clerk asked him where he worked. He responded that he was over at the parking ramp. Apparently assuming that he was a parking attendant at the nearby parking ramp, the sales clerk basically walked away from him and went on about other business, in effect writing him off as a possible purchaser of fine china or crystal. My friend's daughter at that point approached the man and struck up a conversation with him. She asked him open ended questions about what he was looking for and found that he was looking for an addition to his wife's crystal pattern as a gift for their wedding anniversary. Upon further conversation she found that not only did he work at the nearby parking ramp, but he owned it, along with two others in town. She ended up selling him several hundred dollars worth of crystal. She had been willing to treat him like any other customer, whereas the first sales clerk had made an erroneous assumption that, because he looked scruffy, he did not have the money to buy china or crystal.

A similar thing that happens from time to time in retail stores is how to handle a demanding customer who consumes a lot of the sales clerk's time when selecting a small or inexpensive item. Many sales people ignore such a person and write them off as some kind of eccentric. But if these people are served well in their shopping for the small item, many will often come back and make large purchases at a later date. However, if they are treated inhospitably while looking for the inexpensive item, many will never come back to the store again. Remember the demographics discussion and recall the percentage of people spending money at the mass merchandiser—who make very little in annual salary, but who spend on a regular basis.

DEVELOP A CUSTOMER FILE

It is very important to develop a file of who is shopping at a store. This can be very helpful in direct mail advertising and also in analyzing who is buying what in the store. It is fairly easy to identify customers who are paying with checks or credit cards, but the problem comes in identifying cash customers. Stores across the country have used various methods to identify the cash customers. The best methods usually involve getting them to fill out a coupon with their name and address that will give them a chance to win something in an upcoming drawing. Some stores go so far as to collect customer's sizes, and preferences as to styles, colors, etc. Others also collect information such as birthdays of family members and wedding anniversary dates. Some stores have really made their mark by sending reminders to customers about buying gifts for those important dates and, in some cases, actually contacting customers when new merchandise has arrived, especially when it is in their size, style, and color. In general, direct mail advertising is among the most effective advertising methods, especially when it is customized.

An acquaintance of mine tells of his automobile dealership's service department. The service department has a record of all the service they have performed. When a customer drives into the shop, the service manager punches their license plate number into his computer and gets an immediate printout of the service record for his car. By the time the customer gets out of the car, the service manager greets him with his service record in hand. In addition to taking care of the new service tasks, the service manager is often able to suggest other maintenance that needs to be performed. This impressive service is light years ahead of most auto service departments.

DO SOMETHING EXTRA

To make your store stand out from your competition, get in the habit of doing something extra, when appropriate. For example, when people purchase bulky or heavy articles, offer to carry them out to their vehicle. Automobile repair shops which vacuum your car and/or run it through the car wash make many points with customers with extra services. Carpet cleaning companies that call back a week after cleaning your carpet and ask if any stains reappeared and offer to come remove them endear themselves to customers. Many businesses have found ways to offer these little extras and they produce loyal customers.

One reputable clothing store goes out of its way to take care of its customers. The owner usually appears in periodic television ads. His closing line is "Remember, no sale is ever final. We'll see to it that you are completely satisfied, because I'm here and I own the store." That gives a great feeling of confidence to those of who have trouble finding clothes that fit properly. It also contrasts sharply with the stores that post signs that say **"All Sales are Final!"**

EMPOWER YOUR EMPLOYEES

Customers like to do business with store personnel who know their business and have the authority to take care of problems that arise. Customers do not like to do business with employees who do not know store policies and need to get approval from management every time something out of the ordinary comes up. Owners and managers should make sure that employees know store policy and should empower them to take care of all but the most serious problems by using their common sense and making a decision, leaning in favor of the customer when in doubt. From time to time employees with such power will make decisions that the owner/manager may not have made. In such instances, management should stand behind the employee's decision (assuming that the customer is pleased with the outcome). When management feels that an employee has made a serious error, the matter should be discussed so that it will not recur in the future.

I have a friend who took his television set to the service department of his regular consumer electronics and appliance store after it suddenly lost its picture. The young men working in the repair department said they would fix it within two days. My friend could not get back to the shop for a week and, when he asked for his set, the repair people claimed to have no knowledge of it, but started looking around for it. My friend soon spotted it sitting on the counter tuned in to a game show. He said, "Here it is on the counter playing." Upon which one of the repair people said, "Oh, that set, you must have jiggled it when you brought it in. We turned it on and it worked fine so we have been watching it all week." My friend said, "Okay, I'll take it home then." The senior repair man said, "That will be $20 please." My friend offered his credit card even though he was surprised that he was asked to pay for services not rendered. The service people said, "We can't take a credit card unless the amount is at least $25. My friend did not have cash or a check book on him so he left the TV set there while he drove 15 minutes to his home to get his checkbook and 15 minutes back. He said the longer he thought about it the madder he got. When he got back to the store he said, "Did you at least adjust the focus to earn the $20?" To which the senior repairman said, "No, but if you want us to adjust the focus, that will be another $25." That did it for my friend. He grabbed his TV set, left the store and has not been back since. He said that he had spent over $4,000 in the store in the past, and had planned to spend another few thousand dollars in the near future, but he has found another dealer who offers better service.

The above story is an example of employees not having any authority. Their employer is to blame, since he had apparently laid down strict rules for them which they believed they were never to break. Empowered employees would have seen the petty nature of the situation and would have at least allowed the use of the credit card to keep the customer satisfied.

Again Wal-Mart offers an example of how even a large company can empower its associates. A few years ago, I bought a small package of assorted rubber bands at Wal-Mart. This was at a time when they were still placing price stickers on individual items even though they were using scanner checkout and the items were bar coded. The package was plainly marked at 33 cents. When the cashier scanned it, the price came up 37 cents. When I questioned the discrepancy, the cashier quickly sent someone to check the correct price. When the cashier got the correct number, she said, "I'm sorry sir, the correct price on that item is 37 cents." I said, "You mean you are going to charge me 37 cents when it is plainly marked 33 cents?" To which she quickly responded, "Oh no sir, we are going to give it to you free since it was our mistake." She immediately defused me and sent me happily on my way. A more common procedure is to let the customer have the item for the marked price. However, the point I am trying to make is that the cashier had been empowered to make the decisions necessary to keep the customer happy, even if it meant losing a small amount of money.

Communicate with Your Employees

Lack of communication between management and employees is one of the biggest problems in stores of all kinds. Regular store meetings are a good way of improving this communication, but not many stores conduct them.

Company meetings are great settings for educating employees in new products. One hardware store has monthly meetings, and before each meeting, a few employees are given new products to study and use. At the meeting they then explain and demonstrate to the others the operation, benefits and features of the item. This is a very effective method of teaching. As most teachers know, students absorb a little bit of a subject by reading about it. They learn more about it when they actually get hands on experience with the subject matter. But the maximum learning occurs when they have to teach the subject to other students. This also helps eliminate the monotony and boredom associated with some company meetings.

A lawn and garden dealer told me the other day that he hears comments from his employees such as "Oh, no, not another company meeting." He said his employees are happy when he has to cancel a meeting. I suggested he needed to do something to get the employees involved so that they are not just receptors of information, but also dispensers.

Regular store meetings should be held at least once a month. The meetings should be in a non-threatening setting where employees are encouraged to inform management of what they observe customers liking or disliking; what they hear customers asking for that may not now be in stock. They should be told that new products will be arriving or when replacement items will be in stock. Even a large company like Wal-Mart manages to get associates involved in this process by asking them to recommend new products that they believe would be successful. Managers can stock these products on a trial basis, and items that turn out to be popular may sometimes be stocked nationwide. A point system for each participating employee is kept and the winners are rewarded in some way.

QUALITY COMMITMENT STEPS TO BETTER CUSTOMER RELATIONS

Perhaps the most important steps that can be taken in competing with mass merchandisers is to have top quality customer relations. Most local merchants should be able to treat customers in a much more personal and friendly manner than their large competitors. But better customer relations don't just happen. They must be initiated by the owner/manager and must be carried out by everyone working in the business. After bench marking the companies that have the best customer relations, everyone in the company should make a commitment to become as good as or better than the top companies.

1. **Have a Meeting and Commit the Company to Being the Best.** Explain the importance of treating customers as we would like to be treated. Describe what happens when customers are treated inappropriately.

2. **Solicit Complaints and Solve Them Quickly.** Arrange for focus group interviews to identify major problems that exist. Have signs printed that encourage customers to tell you of their concerns. Place advertisements in the local media, encouraging customers to tell you of their problems with your business. Place invitations to complain on your shopping bags, receipts and statements.

3. **Train Employees and Empower Them to Handle Customer Complaints.** This is the most crucial link in the process. Employees must deliver on the promise or you will have even more unhappy customers.

4. **Keep Records of Complaints, Find the Root Causes, and Eliminate Them.** The records should be reviewed weekly to determine problem areas. If you can eliminate the root

cause, you can increase customer satisfaction tremendously.

5. **Invoke the Golden Rule in Your Store Operations.**
   - **Greet customers in a friendly manner.** Acknowledge their presence by excusing yourself momentarily from your current customer, making eye contact, and telling them you will be with them shortly.
   - **Send customers away with a smile.** The last action after checkout should be eye contact, a smile, a thank you for shopping here, and a reminder to let you know if anything is wrong.
   - **Learn how to handle irate customers.** Use the LEAR principle.

     Listen

     Empathize

     Ask questions

     Resolve the problem

6. **Don't Pre-Judge Your Customers.** Treat each customer as though they had the ability to buy out the store, because you may come across one when you least expect it.

7. **Develop a Customer File.** Collect customer's names, addresses, phone numbers. Keep a record of their purchases, their sizes, tastes and preferences. Direct mail to these customers and cue them or family members to merchandise or services appropriate for an upcoming event.

8. **Do Something Extra.** Always place the customer's needs ahead of everything else. Help them carry large parcels to their vehicles. Call back occasionally to check on purchases. Give away small advertising items, especially to children. Offer to gift wrap.

8

IMPROVING THE EFFICIENCY OF YOUR BUSINESS

Companies of all types are in a race to become more efficient than their competitors. Nearly every day we see news accounts of companies laying off various numbers of employees. This is often referred to as down-sizing or right-sizing. Automobile manufacturers are producing cars faster and with fewer people than ever before. Telephone companies are handling more calls faster with fewer people than ever before. This has come about because of the intense competitive pressure of being in a world economy and because of the continuing deluge of new technology that allows us to automate more and more functions.

The competitive "efficiency race" is not only affecting manufacturing and service firms. Retailers are also in a constant battle to become more efficient. The mass merchandisers are continually looking for ways to cut their operating expenses. For example, Wal-Mart's operating expenses in fiscal year 1982 were 19.8% of sales. Operating expenses decreased every year until fiscal year 1994 when they shrunk to 15.3% of sales.

How did Wal-Mart reduce its operating expenses so dramatically? Part of the change was statistical, since the company reports on a consolidated financial statement: as the company adds more low margin stores to its roster (such as Sam's and the Supercenters), the overall operating expense ratio is decreased. However, Wal-Mart itself is continually looking for ways to cut operating costs. Its adoption of technology is unparalleled in the world of retailing. Wal-Mart's satellite communications system and its wide use of computers have reduced distribution cost as was previously described. The practice of conducting training and new product introduction over the satellite system is another big money saver. In addition, the company saves money by being able to precisely monitor and control the temperatures and lighting in their stores from a central location.

Aside from all of those innovative uses of modern technology, Wal-Mart commands a lot of "common sense" in controlling operating costs. One example is involving associates in controlling shrinkage. Another is its abhorrence of waste: they work in an austere headquarters building; they travel by the most economical means possible; they stay at economy motels and hotels; they do not spend a lot of money on fancy stationery; their letterhead is placed on correspondence by a word processor and printed out on each letter.

What can local merchants and small chain operators learn from the example of Wal-Mart to become more efficient? There are many lessons that can be learned. Some of them are listed below.

- Become intimately familiar with your financial ratios.
- Compare your financial ratios to the norms for your type of store.
- Automate your operations wherever feasible.
- Cut costs continually.
- Get your employees involved.

GET TO KNOW YOUR FINANCIAL RATIOS

The best merchants know precisely what their sales have been. They know their gross profit margins. They know their operating expenses, including the percentage for wages, advertising, utilities, etc. They know their net profit margins before and after taxes. In other words, they are *on top of their businesses' operations* and are *always looking for ways to improve them.*

The unfortunate truth is that many other merchants do not want to be bothered with the "details" of "boring things" like financial ratios. As long as they can pay the bills, they do not get concerned. Their accountant or bookkeeper looks after the gory details. But does the accountant or bookkeeper really get concerned about these things? Some do and some don't. It depends on what instructions they have been given by the boss. In truth, only the boss truly understands how to act and react upon a given set of ratios, and the accountant must be instructed to advise the boss with such detail.

Every owner/manager should request a monthly financial statement, and should review it for any extraordinary changes. It is sometimes useful to compare a particular month's figures to the same month a year ago. Even more important, the quarterly statements should be carefully reviewed, since they paint a more comprehensive picture of how the year is going. At the end of each year, the annual report should be analyzed in great detail. The various ratios should be compared to previous year's ratios. One would like to see an improvement. If conditions are deteriorating, the reasons for the decline must be determined.

At a minimum, the owner/manager should become familiar with the following.

- Total sales
- Cost of goods
- Gross profit margin
- Operating expenses, including
  —Wages and salaries
  —Utilities
  —Advertising expenses
  —Travel and transportation expenses

- Net profit before taxes
- Net profit after taxes

If you get engrossed in analyzing your financial ratios, you may want to also review solvency ratios, efficiency ratios and profitability ratios.

COMPARING YOUR FINANCIAL RATIOS

Knowing your own financial ratios doesn't mean much if you don't have a norm with which to compare them. There are a few publications that publish financial ratios for different businesses. Table 8-1 shows 1993 financial ratios from Robert Morris Associates which publishes Annual Statement Summaries for various types of businesses. The summaries in Table 8-1 are the median figure (in the middle) for retail and service businesses. These figures should serve as broad guidelines only since Robert Morris Associates gathers its data from cooperating commercial banks; there is probably not great uniformity in accounting conventions, nor is there any accounting for different sizes of businesses in different geographical areas.

Dun and Bradstreet Company also publishes annual summaries of financial and operating ratios. Its reports tend to focus more on *actual dollar amounts* and less on some of the *key ratios*. However, some owners/managers may find this information useful.

Some businesses belong to trade associations that publish annual financial statement summaries. These are probably more comprehensive and useful than the broader summaries discussed above. Certain trade journals periodically publish financial statement summaries as well. These studies will usually have a much better breakdown of the specific operational expenses, such as wages and salaries, advertising, rent, etc. The National Retail Federation also compiles two industry surveys, *Financial & Operating Results of Retail Stores* and *Merchandising & Operating Results of Retail Stores* (published annually by John Wiley & Sons, Inc.)

If your ratios are within a few percentage points of the Robert Morris figures, you can be satisfied that you are at least "in the ball park." However, if your ratios are several percentage points from

Table 8-1. 1993 Financial Ratios for Retail and Service Businesses

Type of Store	Gross Profit Margin (%)	Operating Expenses (%)	Net Profit Before Tax (%)
Building Supplies			
Building Materials	29.6	25.3	2.2
Paint, Glass, Wallpaper	37.8	35.0	2.4
Hardware	34.9	32.9	1.6
Nursing & Garden Center	38.2	35.2	2.1
General Merchandise			
Department Stores	31.2	29.9	0.6
Variety Stores	38.0	34.3	2.3
Misc. General Merchandise	34.7	31.5	2.6
Food			
Grocery Stores	22.9	21.9	1.1
Retail Bakeries	38.2	35.2	2.1
Automotive Dealers			
Auto & Home Supply	35.6	33.2	1.8
Gasoline Service Stations	19.7	19.2	1.2
Boat Dealers	25.3	23.7	0.6
Recreational Vehicles	19.7	16.9	1.7
Apparel Stores			
Men's & Boys' Clothing	41.9	38.5	2.7
Women's Clothing	40.4	38.2	1.5
Children's & Infants' Wear	37.5	34.7	1.3
Family Clothing	37.7	34.3	2.6
Shoe Stores	39.8	36.5	1.8
Home Furnishings			
Furniture Stores	39.6	36.5	1.8
Floor Covering Stores	33.1	30.7	1.7
Radio, Television & Electronic Stores	35.4	32.6	2.3
Computer & Software Stores	34.6	31.2	2.7
Musical Instrument Stores	42.4	39.0	3
Eating & Drinking Stores			
Eating Places	57.4	52.5	3.5
Misc. Specialty Stores			
Drug Stores	29.9	27.1	2.5
Liquor Stores	21.4	19.9	1.3

Source: Robert Morris Associates *Annual Statement Summaries*

Table 8-1. 1993 Financial Ratios for Retail and Service Businesses (Cont'd)

Type of Store	Gross Profit Margin (%)	Operating Expenses (%)	Net Profit Before Tax (%)
Sporting Goods &			
Bicycle Stores	34.5	31.4	2
Book Stores	37.5	32.6	4.2
Stationery Stores	35.9	33.8	1.7
Jewelry Stores	45.8	41	3.5
Hobby, Toy & Game Shops	39.6	35.4	3.1
Camera & Photo			
Supply Stores	31.5	29	1.8
Gift, Novelty,			
Souvenir Shops	44.4	39.8	3.4
Business Services			
Photocopying &			
Duplicating Services	49.8	43.8	4.6
Commercial Photography	*	93.5	5
Disinfecting & Pest			
Control Services	*	95.9	3.5
Medical Equipment Rental	64.3	52.8	9.2
Equipment Rental &			
Leasing	*	86.2	8.1
Prepackaged Computer			
Software	61.8	54.7	6.1
Photo Finishing			
Laborotories	49.9	43.8	4.7
Auto Repair Services			
Auto Exhaust System			
Repair	*	95.7	2.1
General Auto Repair Shops	*	95.5	3
Refrigeration Service &			
Repair	*	96.5	3.6
Motion Pictures			
Motion Picture Theatres	*	87.9	7.1
Video Tape Rental	*	92.3	5.7

* Incomplete Data

Source: Robert Morris Associates *Annual Statement Summaries*

those in Table 8-1, you should certainly investigate further. Readers are cautioned that the net profit before tax in this table appears to be very low. That is because the owner's draw and/or officers' salaries have already been subtracted, and this is the residual.

Once you become familiar with how your financial and operating ratios compare to industry norms, you need to make a commitment to try to improve them. In particular, good owners and managers are always on the lookout for ways to *reduce operating expenses.* That is one obvious way in which to improve your ratios. The following sections provide more detail.

WAYS TO AUTOMATE YOUR OPERATIONS

One of the ways to improve your operational efficiency is to look for ways to automate. Technology is developing at a rapid rate and is becoming increasingly more affordable. Computers, scanner checkouts, fax machines, and other technology that would have been too costly 10 years ago are now well within the budgets of many small businesses. Desktop computers with enough capacity to handle most of the requirements of small businesses can be purchased at reasonable costs. There is no reason today not to take full advantage of the possibilities for efficiency improvement offered by computerization and automation.

Scanner checkout systems are another way in which small stores can improve efficiency. Several convenience store chains now speed people through the checkout line much faster with the use of scanners.

Trade shows are a good place to view the latest advancements in new technology available to your industry. A trade show will encompass the different brands and models, will offer demonstrations, and is a singular place to gather sales brochures and technical information.

If you do not have a lot of experience with technological equipment, you may want to talk with other merchants who are using the various systems that you are considering. It is important to ensure that you get the right system for you. In particular, computer systems software should be designed to do everything you want it to do and should be user friendly.

If the new equipment you are purchasing is somewhat complex, it may be a good idea to purchase it from a company that will send a representative to your business to help you set up. This person can also train you and others to operate the equipment. It is important to start using the equipment as quickly as possible and to resolve any glitches immediately in order to be most cost-effective. Too many small companies acquire new equipment, but never find the "right time" to begin using it. Consequently, it starts gathering dust, is never really integrated into the system and quickly becomes obsolete.

CUT COSTS CONTINUALLY

Small companies must continually cut costs. Every procedure in the business should be reviewed to determine if there is a more economical way to do it. The old addage, "We've always done it that way," should be challenged every day. Innovation is a daily process for the Wal-Marts who are eating up your market share, and innovation should be a daily practice in order to stay ahead of the game.

The largest savings can be found in the areas of shipping, transportation and cooperative buying. If you can successfully automate some of your operations, then there may also be major cost savings if you can operate with less people. Scanners at checkout counters, for example, save labor by not only speeding up checkout, but by eliminating labor involved in placing price stickers on individual items.

There are dozens of small ways to cut costs—from fixing leaky faucets, to recycling waste paper, to consolidating trips for supplies and controlling shrinkage.

In a free enterprise economic system, businesses that are inefficient or wasteful will not succeed. Therefore, elimination of inefficiencies and waste should become an everyday habit, by both owners and employees.

GET YOUR EMPLOYEES INVOLVED

It is difficult to achieve real cost cutting without the intense interest and cooperation of your employees. One way to get them interested is to offer a profit sharing system. In order to do so, financial information would have to be shared with employees on a regular basis. Each year, a target profit should be established (higher than the previous year) and employees should know the percentage of profit they will receive if the goals are met. This type of incentive is essential to get employees fully involved in cost cutting.

Some companies also make direct awards to employees for suggestions that save money through improved operations or other cost-cutting measures. In such programs, it is imperative that the awards be made in a fair and equitable manner. For example, when one employee submits a suggestion that is implemented and it can be documented that it saved the company a certain amount of money, the employee should receive a monetary award. The amount should be set *before* the program is implemented. For example, a company owner may choose to award half of the first year savings to the employee up to a maximum of $10,000.

It is important to investigate that an employee has not "borrowed" the idea from another employee or that other employees might have contributed in some way. It is because of the difficulty in assigning savings amounts and in determining the originator of the ideas that many companies have dropped this type of program in favor of profit sharing for all employees.

QUALITY COMMITMENT STEPS

In order to be successful in today's economy, companies of all types must continually become more efficient. Make a vow to start streamlining your company right away, using the following suggestions as guidelines.

1. **Get to Know Your Financial Ratios.** Many business owners do not like to get involved in the financial end of the

business. However, financial ratios are the vital signs of your business. You desperately need to stay on top of your *gross profit margins*, your *operating expenses*, and your *profit margins*. Furthermore, you need to compare to previous years to determine trends. If you are not improving these margins, you are going backward and probably will not be in business for much longer.

2. **Compare Your Financial Ratios to Industry Standards.** Reference publications provide norms for different types of businesses. Get to know them. Check with your trade association to see if financial ratios are available for your industry. When your ratios are out of line, look for causes and take immediate action to remedy the problem.

3. **Look for Ways to Automate Your Operation.** Improved technology is the "wave" of the future. If you do not presently own and make efficient use of computers, scanners, and fax machines, investigate their feasibility and implement them if at all possible. Today I checked on my phone bill that got lost in the mail via computerized billing over the telephone. I found out when my last payment was received, the amount paid and my current balance without ever talking to a human being. How many people and how long would this have taken a few years ago?

4. **Cut Costs Continually.** There are dozens of ways that costs can be cut on a daily basis, including turning off unneeded lights, recycling paper, streamlining transportation, etc.

5. **Get Your Employees Involved.** Instill the cost cutting mentality in all employees and implement a profit sharing plan as an incentive for finding ways of operating more efficiently.

SUMMARY

A company can do all the right things with respect to marketing, merchandising, service and customer relations, but if it is not run *efficiently*, it is doomed to failure. These five steps provide a roadmap to improving your company's efficiency. They have been used successfully by many of today's profitable businesses.

9

IMPLEMENTING THE CHANGES

If a company is in pretty good shape overall, it is fairly easy to implement minor changes that will improve operations, but it is not easy for a company with major problems to turn itself around or to make big changes in operating procedures. If the owner/manager of such a company walks in one morning and announces, "Okay, we're going to shape this place up and make it a quality company by next week," the employees would probably think that he or she had gone off the deep end. There are no easy ways to do it, but it can be done. No matter how it is done, if it is to be effective, employees must be involved in every step of the process.

The overall process should probably begin with a company meeting at which the boss announces that she or he believes that the time has come to make some substantial changes in the company. The reason for changes should be articulated, whether it's because of the recent opening of nearby mass merchandisers, due to changing trends in the industry, because the company is not making a profit, or because the company has simply gotten behind the times. If owners and managers do not feel comfortable in leading such a meeting, sometimes bringing in an outside "expert" can be effective. The steps described in this chapter offer one procedure that could be used to turn a company around, although there are probably many variations of this that would also work.

1. Assess the company's strengths and weaknesses.
2. Assess the strengths and weaknesses of the competition.
3. Determine a course of action.
4. Check the progress and make mid-course corrections.

ASSESS THE COMPANY'S STRENGTHS AND WEAKNESSES

Input for assessing a company's strengths and weaknesses should come from customers and from company personnel. If a company is truly customer-driven, the utmost attention should be given to finding out what customers really think of the business. This could be done through a comprehensive customer survey or through focus group interviews. Although customer surveys are more scientific in that random samples of customers can be drawn and exact values assigned to their responses, focus group interviews are the most direct way to find out what customers really think about your business. This general process was described in the chapter on marketing. However, in this case the focus groups would be assembled for the sole purpose of assessing the strengths and weaknesses of *your* business.

CUSTOMER FOCUS GROUPS

Four or five diverse groups of people representative of your customer base should be assembled by an outside expert. Each group could consist of eight to ten people. As with the community interview, each group should be interviewed separately for two to three hours. The big difference between these interviews and the community interviews is that the groups will be focusing on your business alone. The groups can be asked about specific policies, practices, promotions, etc. In addition, they can be asked a lot of "what if" questions about new policies or practices that you may be considering. Therefore, it is essential that owners/managers sit down with the interviewer and construct a list of the specific questions they want answered. These would include finding the focus groups' opinion of present operating procedures and policies. In addition, owners/managers should inform the interviewer of any new policies, practices or procedures they are considering, so that the interviewer can determine the reaction of the panelists.

In bigger cities, it is common to conduct these focus group sessions with the owners/managers looking on behind a one-way mirror, but this is generally not recommended. For one thing it does not take a genius panel member to figure out that someone is probably watching and listening behind the mirror. This can inhibit open and honest dialog. Also, some owners who watch these interviews become personally offended by remarks made by certain customers and hold a grudge against them.

It is better to conduct the focus groups in private and record the remarks in the most efficient way. A court reporter might be a very effective way of recording these conversations. Court reporters are quiet, unobtrusive, fast and efficient. They also have the ability to momentarily stop the interview to clarify any unclear statement. However, the transcripts should be edited to remove any remarks that may identify a panelist. It is very important that panelists remain anonymous.

Different interviewers may have different methods of conducting the focus groups. One good method is to open the discussion by stating the purpose of the inteviews, indicating that the company is trying to improve its operations and stating that the panel members will serve a very important function by giving their honest opinions. The early questions should be aimed at getting some general impressions of the participants' image of the store. For example questions should be asked about:

- Exterior appearance
- Ease of parking
- Interior appearance

- Layout of the store
- Interior displays

After the participants start adjusting to the interviewer and the routine, then more specific subjects can be addressed.

Selection

Each group should be asked for their views of the store's selection. The specific questions will depend on the type of store, but would generally cover the following.

- Completeness
- Colors
- Styles
- Models
- Sizes
- Brands

Pricing

The discussion on the store's pricing structure should be relatively unstructured in order to find participants' general impressions of the price levels. In some cases, the owner/manager may want participants' perceptions of the prices of certain items, in which case, specific questions can be asked. It may also be a good idea to put together a list of price-sensitive items, then go through the list one item at a time to determine the participants' perceptions of their relative appropriateness.

In addition, participants should be asked for their opinions on the manner in which prices are displayed. Do they like it, do they dislike it? What improvements would they like?

Opening Hours

Participants should be asked if they know the current operating hours of the business. They should then be asked if these hours meet their needs. Some consensus should be reached as to the optimal opening hours. The owner/operator may want to test some proposed changes in opening times on the groups to get their reactions.

Return Policies

Participants should be queried to see if they understand the store returns policy. They should be asked if they are satisfied with the current policies. If not, their expectations should be determined.

In-store Signs

Photographs of signage or actual signs should be shown to get the reaction of the panel members. Do they view the signs as helpful and attractive? What change, if any, would they like to see?

Advertising

Samples of the store's advertising should be shown. Panel members should be asked for their reactions to the various ads. Suggested changes should be solicited.

Customer Relations

The opinions of participants should be sought regarding the manner in which they are treated when doing business with the store. Both praise and horror stories should be accepted.

Checkout Procedures

Panel members should be asked of their impressions of the efficiency of the checkout and whether it is done in a friendly manner.

Competency of Employees

Participants should be asked for their opinions of employee competency. Are they knowledgeable? Are they empowered to handle most problems? Are they friendly?

As was mentioned earlier, the owner/manager should submit any specific questions that she or he would like answered. Any potential changes in policies or operating procedures could also be tested for reactions from the panels.

The answers gathered from focus group interviews such as these are invaluable in determining current strengths and weaknesses. Sometimes some of the problem areas can be corrected easily and with a minimum of expense. Others may require major resources to correct.

ASSESS THE STRENGTHS AND WEAKNESSES OF THE COMPETITION

If your company is to truly become among the best, it is imperative to research your competition. This is where the benchmarking procedures described earlier are best employed.

Benchmarking

Benchmarking involves listing the characteristics of your business that are important to the customer. After the list is compiled, the major task is finding the competitors that are considered the best in class with respect to each characteristic. For example, in-store signage would probably be on everyone's list of characteristics. The problem is in finding the store that has the best in-store signage. Several sources could be tapped. For example, the focus groups could be asked of their opinions of the best store. Certainly your employees and friends could be asked for their opinions of which store is the best. Salespeople who call on your business are also a valuable source of this information, since they see many stores and can easily make comparisons. If you have a parent company, it can often help you in finding the best in your class.

Once you have found the companies that are operating in the best manner, then, if at all possible, visits should be made to these stores to see first hand how the companies operate. Whenever possible, you should include your employees as companions on these visits. In some cases, employees alone may visit the best-in-class stores.

After you and your employees have had a chance to see how the best stores operate, then it will be necessary to put together a plan for meeting or exceeding the stores that are now considered the best. In some cases, compromises may need to be made when there are financial constraints or space limitations. The toughest task is carrying out the changes in a logical and orderly fashion.

Assembling the List of Characteristics

In assembling the list of important characteristics, the first step is to use some common sense and draw upon your own experience and knowledge. You may find several items from the focus group interviews. Every store's list will be different, but some common items include the following, listed in random order.

- Store operating hours
- Store signage
- In-store displays
- Services offered
- Special order procedures
- Layout of store
- Checkout procedures
- Returns policies
- Friendliness of store personnel
- Knowledge of store personnel
- Advertising copy
- Pricing levels
- Store lighting
- Merchandise mix
- End cap displays
- Cross merchandising techniques

- Training of employees
- Customer relations

Once the list is assembled, it should be prioritized. It is important that employees be involved in this process. They may have some additions or deletions to offer. The priorities should be ordered according to what is most important to the customer, not in the order of ease of accomplishment.

Determining the Best-In-Class

Once the prioritized list is completed, it is important to identify the stores that are considered the best in each of the categories. Make several copies of the list. Let each employee suggest the best-in-class stores. Pass the lists to salespeople and to parent company personnel, and ask them to help in listing the best stores. Once everyone has had a chance to respond, compile a consensus list.

You will probably find that two or three competing stores are considered the best in several of the categories. This makes life simple, since fewer trips are needed for store visits. When there appears to be little consensus on certain categories, then compile the most frequently listed store names and go through the process again to see if consensus can be reached.

Visit the Best Stores

Plans should be made to visit the various best-in-class stores as soon as possible. If you have no employees or very few employees, you are probably the designated visitor. However, if you have several employees working for you, it is a good idea to split up the duties among them according to characteristic.

When you find that one competing store is best in most of the characteristics, you can make the visit a fun outing. Some small business owners have loaded four or five of their top employees into a car or van and visited a large competing store for a half day. Each person is assigned various things to investigate. In some cases, the owner gives a modest amount of money to each employee so that they can purchase various items and witness first hand the way customers are treated. Each person should also be on the lookout for any new ideas they may pick up in the competitor's store.

Develop the Plan

As soon as possible after the visits to the best stores, a store meeting should be held to compare notes and articulate the findings. The discussions should include what will be necessary to make your store as good or better than the stores that were visited. A plan should be put together, listing in chronological order the logical sequence of events to accomplish your goals. A reasonable time table should be established for completing each of the actions.

TAKE ACTION TO CHANGE

Ultimately, changes must be made in order to become a top rate store. There is a lot of merit in making some of the easier changes first, especially those that customers will notice. For example, a good first step would be to conduct some intensive training on customer relations. When employees start treating customers better than they have been accustomed to, they start to notice that something is happening. The positive results should encourage store personnel to get on with the next steps.

A good second step for many stores is to improve the returns policy. Basically, the intent is to have a no hassle policy, where the customer goes away satisfied. If your store is to be among the best, this is a necessity, because this is what customers have come to expect.

Another action that could be taken early in the process is to develop a list of price-sensitive items and mark the prices on them down to the level of the mass merchandisers.

Store operating hours is something that could also be changed early in the process. Once the appropriate hours are determined, then a regular advertising campaign is necessary for a while to make the public aware of the changes.

Other changes may require a lot more planning. For example, if the merchandise mix is to be changed or if the store is to be re-fixtured or re-set, a lot of planning and probably substantial money will be needed.

Throughout the process, regular store meetings should be held to keep everyone abreast of the progress. Any problems should be addressed and solved as soon as possible. Feedback should be sought from customers throughout the process. Comment cards and informal discussion should help determine customer response.

10

TEAM BUILDING

Whenever anyone asked Sam Walton what the most important factor was in molding Wal-Mart into such a successful chain, his inevitable response was "the associates": Wal-Mart's name for its employees. Walton was keenly aware that the best policies and intentions are ineffective without the enthusiastic cooperation and participation of the employees. Wal-Mart executives are fond of saying that their associates are "ordinary people performing extraordinary deeds." That is probably a fairly accurate assessment. Many of the associates who work for Wal-Mart are not highly educated, but they seem to take pride in their work and seem to be very customer oriented. Since the company is hiring from the same labor pool as all other local businesses, and since they pay approximately the same wages, how is it that their employees perform better than many of their competing businesses?

Home Depot is the premier building materials chain in the country. Founder Bernie Marcus is also often quoted as saying that it is the associates that make Home Depot such a successful business. However, Home Depot's strategy with respect to employees differs considerably from those of the discount general merchandise stores such as Wal-Mart, Kmart and Target. Home

Depot pays substantially higher wages to hire recognized experts and experienced people in their various departments such as plumbing, electrical, lawn and garden, etc. The company often displays photographs of its employees at the entry to the store and lists any licenses they may have, plus their experience level. But we know that money alone does not motivate employees to perform at a high level. So what is it that accounts for the high level of service offered by Home Depot employees?

The Disney Company hires thousands of people, most of them fairly young, to operate their various theme parks. The performance of Disney employees has been highly acclaimed by various experts on personnel management, and has been observed by millions of people who have visited their parks and witnessed it first hand. What is it that causes Disney personnel to perform at a higher level than most of their competitors?

The three companies cited above, along with many other successful companies, must be doing some things differently with respect to their employees to achieve such enviable results. Officials of each company would probably use slightly different words to describe their personnel management techniques, but most of them would include principles to similar those listed below.

- Hire the right people in the first place.
- Give them extensive initial training and education.
- Continue training and education on a regular basis.
- Develop effective communication methods.
- Instill in them a strong customer orientation.
- Each of these categories of personnel management is discussed separately in the sections that follow.

HIRE THE RIGHT PEOPLE IN THE FIRST PLACE

Many of the problems with employees could be eliminated by hiring the right people in the first place. Many companies do not have effective methods for evaluating potential employees. There are several methods for attracting and evaluating potential employees. A good place to start is to educate yourself on proper hiring procedures in more detail than will be offered here. There are books on the subject that can be found in local libraries, at community colleges, at Small Business Development Centers, at employment services offices, etc. Also, seminars are conducted fairly regularly in many towns and cities across the country by colleges, universities and consultants. This section provides an outline of proper hiring techniques in order to start you on your research.

Advertise the Job Properly

Make sure that your job announcement is attractive, accurate, meets government equal opportunity criteria, and is listed in the right places. Some jobs are not as attractive as others, but each job announcement should be well thought out to emphasize the positive aspects, including benefits and potential for advancement. For example, a stocker position is not a particularly glamorous position, but an ad could state that it is a great way to learn the basics of retailing and could lead to eventual promotion to management or operating your own business.

The medium used to advertise new positions should be tailored to the job type and the type of person you hope to hire. For example, if you are looking for an experienced person, this would usually mean someone who is older, who likely would read a local newspaper. Therefore an advertisement in the local newspaper would be desirable. If you are hiring at the entry level and envision the candidates as younger people, it may be more appropriate to advertise on radio stations that young people listen to. Of course, signs in the store entryway or on bulletin boards are always appropriate.

If you want to search for candidates beyond the local area, you can list your jobs with the state department of employment services. Most of these departments make statewide distribution with on line computer listings. Employment agencies may be a consideration for some positions. Of course, it is always good to pass the word along to existing employees in case they have friends or acquaintances who may be interested.

Use a Good Job Application Form

It is important to get pertinent and accurate information on job candidates. The use of a good application form can be very helpful in recording education, experience, aspirations, and so on. Employment advisory firms offer standard application forms , or you can make your own. If you devise your own application forms, have them critiqued by experts to make sure that they meet government equal opportunity and affirmative action requirements.

Interview the Candidates

After applications are reviewed and possible candidates are decided upon, the leading candidates should be invited to the store or work site for an interview. The interviewer should be completely familiar with Equal Employment Opportunities Procedures and avoid questions that violate these rules.

The interview should be amiable and mutually instructive. Most interviewers keep the conversation light initially, and gradually lead into matters of education, experience and aspirations. The candidates should be shown the work area and given a detailed explanation of the job requirements and your expectations. In addition to inquiring about qualifications, the interviewer should also be evaluating the attitude of the candidate. Studies have found that having a positive attitude and being a team player are two of the most important attributes found in successful employees.

Check References

One of the last things an employer should do before extending an offer to a candidate is check his or her references. Written references are traditional, but whenever possible references should be contacted and interviewed in person or over the phone. By talking to references, the employer can get more detail than is usually provided in writing. In addition, various points can be elaborated upon or further explained.

Hire on a Probationary Basis

It is customary to hire new people on a probationary basis today. For retail employees, the probationary period should be relatively short, for example three to six months. A probationary period allows an employer to evaluate new employees to measure their progress and to determine if they will fit into the organization. The probationary period also provides incentive for new employees to prove themselves and to learn their jobs quickly and well.

INITIAL TRAINING AND EDUCATION

As soon as new employees are hired, they should be trained in a well thought out and thorough manner. The initial training should include at least the following.

- Complete tour of the store or work facility
- Introduction to all company personnel
- Training on company policy
- Training on specific details of the job
- Training on general aspects of business practices
- On-the-job-training

Complete Tour of the Store or Work Facility

It is important that new employees be given a complete tour of the business facilities by the owner or manager. Businesses that make no plans for an official store tour, that assign an inexperienced employee to escort the new employee on his or her initial tour, convey the impression that the owner/manager does not consider the new employee important enough to receive a few minutes of his/her time. In addition, when new employees are given orientation tours by inexperienced employees, erroneous information can be passed along. New employees need to see the entirety of the operation from the receiving and storage area to the store aisles, to the office area. The new employee should understand how his or her job fits into the overall scheme of things.

The initial tour of the facilities is a great time to introduce new employees to present store employees. At each introduction, the new employee's position should be explained and current employees asked to explain their duties and responsibilities.

Training on Company Policy

During the initial orientation tour, company policies should be explained. However, it is very important that businesses have a written policy manual. For larger companies this may be a sizeable loose leaf booklet, but for smaller firms it could be something as simple as a four or five page pamphlet. At a minimum, the following items should be explained.

- Company philosophy
- Hours of operation and reporting hours
- Procedures for reporting an illness or family emergency
- Dress code, including uniforms or badges that are to be worn
- Standards of behavior to include smoking, gum chewing, language, etc.
- The company's returns policy
- Procedures for greeting customers
- Telephone procedures and etiquette
- Procedures for dealing with irate customers
- Procedures for dealing with suspected shoplifters
- Procedures for making suggestions
- Company benefits, including specific information on medical care
- Procedures for handling in-store fires, accidents or other emergencies

New employees should be informed that after a reasonable period of time to read the policy manual, two weeks for example, they will be given a test on the subject. The test should cover the most important policy areas and new employees should be allowed to re-take the test until they get all answers correct. This procedure helps to reinforce the importance of understanding company policies and ensures that new employees do not have erroneous ideas about it. As policies are revised or added, employees should be informed and changes made to policy manuals.

Specific Job Training

Training new employees on the specific aspects of their job is one of the most important ways to get them "off on the right foot," and yet many businesses do not devote enough attention to the matter. Nearly everyone has run into situations where new employees have been thrust into the everyday "hustle-bustle" of business without proper training. It is a very frustrating experience for both the employees and for the customers. I offer the following anecdote as an example:

Last year while travelling on Interstate 74 in Illinois, I witnessed a situation where a young lady was thrust into such a job without proper training. I had stopped at an interchange for gasoline. When I went inside to pay for the gasoline, two people were ahead me in line for the cash register. After a few minutes, I noticed that the line was not moving. It soon became obvious that the cashier did not know how to operate the cash register. She made a call to someone to find out the procedure while dealing with the man at the head of the line. Finally, she got him checked out. Then the women ahead of me offered a credit card for payment of her gasoline, which confused the cashier again, precipitating another telephone call for assistance. As the cashier tried to ring up the credit card sale, the customer ahead of me suddenly decided that she also wanted to buy two packs of cigarettes, which added more confusion and caused the cashier to make another phone call. By this time there were 10 or 12 customers lined up behind me, grumbling and adding to the pressure on the cashier. After trying for another few minutes to incorporate the cigarettes into the sale, the cashier finally said, "I'm sorry. I can sell you the gasoline, but I can't sell you the cigarettes because I can't figure how to ring them up." The frustrated customer ahead of me said, "Well, what am I supposed to do about the cigarettes?" To which, the cashier responded, "I don't know, maybe you can buy them across the street."

The above story exposes a more negative side of American service businesses. Of course there are many good companies who serve customers well most of the time, but unfortunately, all too many do a poor job of training their people and serving their customers. Obviously the employee discussed above should have been trained on every aspect of operating the cash register, including having an overseer nearby for the first few days of actually serving customers. In addition, she should have been given the authority, that in the event that she could not ring up an item on the cash register, to take the money, make a note, and worry about ringing it up properly at a later time. With the proper initial training, horror stories such as the above can be avoided. This training should include the following plus anything else that is appropriate for the specific job.

Operation of Machines

New personnel should be given extensive training on any kind of machines or equipment that they will be operating within the business. A knowledgeable person within the company should be assigned the task of teaching new employees how to operate these machines in a safe and efficient manner. Sometimes the learning process can take place through merely demonstrating how the machine or equipment should be operated, and then letting the new employee try it several times until he or she seems competent and confident. When the new employee actually starts using the equipment or machinery on the job, however, the trainer should be nearby in case anything goes wrong. With some complex equipment such as computers, electronic cash registers and others, it is usually helpful to give the operator's manual to new employees to read in their spare time. Also with more complex equipment and machines, new employees should be given the chance to spend an appropriate period conducting "dry run" practices before serving "live" customers.

Product Knowledge

New employees should know as much as possible about the products they will be selling or servicing before they actually have customer contact. In many ways, today's customers are less knowledgeable than ever before on many of the products or services they purchase mainly because they have less and less time to spend in learning about products. Many products today such as automobiles, computers, television sets, lawn mowers and many others are much more complex than ever before. Many customers rely only on ratings from consumer magazines. For this reason many customers seek out salespeople who really know what they are selling and can explain it in a meaningful manner. Since more and more salespeople do not know the product they are selling, you are adding value to your store by providing knowledgeable salespeople.

I have found automobiles salespeople who do not know such basic things as the cubic feet of trunk space in a car, whether the valve train is driven by belt or by chain, what is covered in the warranty, how often the timing belt has to be changed, whether the valves have to be adjusted, etc. It is hard to make a $20,000 purchase from someone who knows less about the product than the average young teenager. How, then, do we educate new employees so that they learn the essentials of the products they are selling and maintain the enthusiasm for continually learning more? The following suggestions are offered.

- **Make a list of sources the employee should study.** Provide operator's manuals, company promotional materials, trade journals, consumer magazines and ask employees to learn as much as possible from these sources.

- **Encourage employees to ask questions of company sales representatives.** Usually, company representatives know the specific details of the products they are selling.
- **Encourage employees to ask questions of service personnel.** Nothing conveys the workings of products better than a presentation by a service person over the disassembled items.
- **Encourage employees to use the products whenever possible.** In this way employees can experience firsthand how the product works and then can more convincingly explain it to customers.
- **Ask customers for their experiences with the product.** When a salesperson can report that "my customers use this product in this way and have had great success" he or she gains credibility with a new customer.

CONTINUE TRAINING ON A REGULAR BASIS

The successful companies take every opportunity to train their people on a regular basis throughout their tenure. However, many owners of small businesses look only at the short run and see continued training as an expense instead of an investment in the future. One example is the attendance at trade shows or dealer meetings sponsored by parent companies. Generally, companies that have sent their employees to the meetings are some of the better companies in the parent organization. The owners and managers of these companies want their employees to learn as much as possible and to be exposed to any new ideas that may be around. Conversely, representatives of some of the poorer companies within parent organizations seldom, if ever, send their employees to any kind of training. With the rapid change in technology today, products change frequently and the challenge to employees to keep up with them becomes even greater. Continual, ongoing training is the only way to keep employees apprised of new developments, and therefore remain competitive in your marketplace. The following ideas are offered to help owners and managers provide continual training for their employees.

Encourage the Reading of Trade Journals

Trade journals are an invaluable source of information concerning the latest trends in the industry. They usually feature new products, often giving specifications, along with benefits and features. Nothing hurts salespeoples' credibility more than a customer knowing about new products that salespeople have not even heard about. If they are made readily available, employees can read about new developments in consumer magazines, newspapers or trade journals. Such publications should be placed at sales counters and lounge areas, and employees should be encouraged to read them.

Send Employees to Trade Shows

Every trade show I've attended has spurred at least one new idea, and usually many more. The same is true for employees who attend such shows. However, as was described above, too many business owners do not send their employees to such shows. Certainly, you cannot send every employee to every show, but you can send them on a rotational basis, sending one or two this year and another one or two next year. The benefits extend beyond just seeing new products at the show and may include:

• **An increase in self esteem and confidence.** When employees are sent to trade shows, most start feeling more a part of the team. They start believing that "if the boss thinks enough of me to send me to this meeting he or she must think that I am an important part of this business." Also, the break from the routine of their duties at the business can afford them the opportunity to think more globally about the business and industry.

• **An opportunity to interact with associates from other business.** Many trade show attendees report that one of the biggest values they receive from attending is the interaction with their peers from other businesses in other parts of the country. By getting to know each other and by trading stories on business practices, they often get new ideas that they take home and adopt.

- **An opportunity to be exposed to the ideas of professional speakers.** Trade shows usually feature presentations by presidents of companies, celebrities, consultants and often by successful dealer representatives. The subjects of these presentations range from the future of the industry to motivation, management, marketing, customer relations and providing better service. Employees may get some new ideas from these presentations or, in some cases, may merely receive reenforcement that the practices they are now employing are the proper ones.

Encourage the Viewing of Video Tapes

There are a multitude of videotapes available today and many are of very good quality, as contrasted to a few years ago when many were rather amateurish. Many companies today produce high quality video tapes of their products, showing technical features, as well as benefits and features. These are *must* viewing for store sales personnel. The video format for learning new product information is especially effective because a video portrays an expert making the presentation and utilizes images, color, motion and sound to illustrate product features. All of these elements are effective in holding the attention of the viewer. In addition, good video tapes are available on the everyday skills of dealing with customers, treating subjects such as:

- Customer relations
- Salesmanship
- Good telephone practices
- Time management
- Principles of good service

For those company officials who feel that they cannot afford to purchase these video tapes, other alternatives are available. In particular, nearly every public university and community college has a film library and many offer them for rental for a short period of time at a very nominal fee. In fact, most film libraries have inter-library loan agreements, where they can obtain video tapes from other institutions if they do not have them in stock.

DEVELOP EFFECTIVE COMMUNICATIONS AMONG COMPANY PERSONNEL

Throughout North America, my studies have shown that communications within small companies are not very effective. Small companies generally lack formal mechanisms for exchanging ideas, news, and policies between and among management and the other workers. The following anecdote illustrates this point. When I was growing up in a small town in Illinois, my dad operated a farm machinery business. One of my uncles was the "parts man" and took care of the bookkeeping. Quite often I would stop by the store after school and the first person I usually encountered was my uncle Paul. My usual greeting was, "Hi Paul, what's going on?" His standard response usually was, "beats the heck out of me, nobody ever tells me anything." Unfortunately, I think that response or some variation of it is what you would get from the majority of small business employees across the country. This trend stems from the fact that owners and managers of small businesses have a great reluctance to share information they consider confidential, such as sales levels, profit margins, etc. Even worse, they fail to use the great resources they have: the minds of their employees. Employees are on the front lines and hear on a daily basis what customers are saying about products, policies and other important issues. Yet many owners/managers never take the time to solicit ideas or suggestions from the employees. The following suggestions for improving company communications are offered.

- Regular company meetings
- A periodic company newsletter
- An annual company meeting
- Sponsorship of league teams
- Frequent company social outings

Regular Company Meetings

One of the simplest methods of improving communications is to institute a regular company meeting. Ideally, the meetings should be held at least once a month and all employees should attend. Naturally, there is some resistance to this concept. Some owner/ managers will think of every excuse under the sun as to why a regular meeting will not work. For example I had a store owner verbally attack me a few months ago when I suggested this alternative. He said, "We stay open from 8:00 a.m. to 8:00 p.m. from Monday through Saturday. How in the hell do you expect us to find time for a company meeting?" Before I could answer, another owner responded by saying, "We stay open those same hours and on the first Monday of each month, I have everybody come in at 7:30 a.m. for a one-half hour company meeting." The complaining owner said, "How do you get them to come in without paying them?" The response from the second owner was, "I pay them." That was about more than the first owner could take. He could not imagine that someone would actually pay their employees for an extra half hour just so that they could attend a meeting. In fact, he apparently got so upset that he walked out of the seminar.

The first owner was taking the short view, looking only at the immediate costs, while the second owner was taking the longer view, anticipating the payoff offered by having well informed employees who felt a part of the team.

The minimal issues that should be covered in a company meeting are as follows:

- How the company is doing: how much sales and profits are up and/or down
- Any changes in company policy
- Any problems as seen by management
- Any upcoming expansions, closings, mergers, etc.
- Any new products being introduced
- Any problems as seen by employees
- Employee suggestions for the good of the company

Periodic Company Newsletters

Company newsletters are very effective communications devices and are fairly easy to produce with the help of desktop computers and desktop publishing. Many companies produce weekly newsletters. Newsletters can update employees on important happenings between monthly meetings. They can also bring a personal touch and convey a family atmosphere to company personnel by announcing awards, births, anniversaries, weddings and training courses completed.

Annual Company Meetings

Unfortunately, very few private companies conduct an annual company meeting. However, an annual meeting seems to be a very effective means of assessing last year's accomplishments and looking forward to the upcoming year. Several years ago, at a national agribusiness conference, a small Illinois-based company won the national award for the best managed small company in the country. The owner of the company was invited to tell the audience how he had accomplished this. He related the following details:

> The owner said his success began with the annual company meeting. The business was closed down for one day while all company personnel, including the salespeople, truck drivers, secretaries and even the janitor, all attended the meeting. The first order of business was to go over the financial results from last year, including sales, costs of goods, expenses, and profits. This was compared to the previous year, and apparently nobody slept through this since they had intense interest in financial ratios. This was because at the previous year's meeting the group had reached a consensus as to the sales and other financial goals for the next year. They knew that if they reached that goal, two or three of them would receive a free vacation to some island paradise. The two or three people would be those whose names appeared at the top of a list. Apparently the list, when initially constructed, placed employees in order of seniority, regardless of position. As new people were hired their name went on

the bottom of the list and, by seniority, they worked their way to the top over a period of time.

Audience members had a lot of questions for the owner of this small Illinois company. Someone asked, "Why a vacation? Why don't you just give them money?" The owner replied that by giving them a vacation it was something they would remember for the rest of their lives, whereas if he gave them money, they would probably pay some bills and it would be quickly forgotten. Someone else asked, "Why do you include the secretaries, the truck drivers and the janitor at the annual meeting? Why not just include the sales personnel?" To this the owner responded, "I want every person in the company to know exactly what is going on and to have a say in what the goals are and to share in the rewards of reaching the goals." He said, "If the secretaries, truck drivers and janitors know that we are shooting for $3 million in sales this year, they will put a little extra effort in their work and in their dealings with customers, all of which makes the company better and helps our chances of reaching the goals."

Not all small companies can offer free vacations to their employees. But certainly they could hold some sort of annual meeting to review how last year went and to set some goals for next year. Unfortunately, many small business owners feel very strongly that this is strictly confidential information. This is indeed unfortunate, because it keeps the employees in the dark and precludes them from getting involved in setting and reaching goals. As time goes on, more and more businesses of all sizes will move to some form of profit sharing. Information sharing and profit sharing foster a team spirit and encourage all employees to work harder to achieve company goals.

Sponsorship of League Teams

This may seem more of a social item and not worthy of including in a list of things to help increase communications. However, when employees get together on a regular basis to bowl, play softball or participate in other organized events, they get to know each other better. In addition, they may discover that they have the same problems at work, and that they can work together to solve them. In general, these types of events develop comradery and should be encouraged.

Frequent Company Social Outings

Again, this may not seem like an appropriate item to include in a section on communications, but annual holiday dinners or annual company picnics have the effect of building teamwork and linking personnel together as part of the company family. Employees get to know other employees and their families better, which helps to create a better level of understanding and appreciation for each other. It has been my observation that companies that play together, also work well together.

Instill a Strong Customer Orientation

Companies that are successful over the long run are those that meet the true wants and needs of their customers. This message has to be delivered by owners/managers both to new employees and to existing employees on a frequent and consistent basis. Stu Leonard's, the hugely successful dairy/grocery in Connecticut, is often cited as the epitome of promoting the principle of customer orientation. Stu Leonard's two basic laws of customer treatment are set in stone (literally) in the front of their stores. Rule one is "The customer is always right." Rule two is "When you think the customer is wrong, refer back to rule one."

Unfortunately, many small merchants refuse to accept the premise that the customer is always right. Of course, we all know that customers are not always right, but if we want them to come back again, we need to treat them as though they are. This begins with the boss instilling in the employees a real concern for the customer. This can be reinforced periodically through training sessions. The following is a partial list of skills that should be covered.

- Greeting the customer
- Listening to the customer to determine needs
- Learning how to handle unusual circumstances
- Learning to go the "extra mile" for the customer

Most of these skills can be learned and rehearsed in company meetings or in informal employee groups. Employees should be asked to discuss their own personal experiences in other stores. For example they should be asked for the best and the worst examples of the skills being discussed. They may also want to volunteer a problem they have had in their own experience and ask for suggested responses.

Greeting the Customer

An easy way to start a training session on greeting customers is to ask employees to describe the worst case they have seen in other stores of customers being improperly greeted. Here's an example from a consumer electronics store:

I was looking for a language translator computer that can be carried on a trip abroad. As I entered the store, two middle-aged employees were standing inside the doorway. They were in the middle of a "gripe session" and neither paid any attention to me. They were complaining about the hours assigned them, about the preferential treatment that another employee was getting and the ineptness of the boss. After listening to their complaints for awhile, I finally interrupted and asked for directions to the translators. One employee sullenly led me to a corner of the store, all the while continuing his gripe session with his fellow employee over his shoulder. After we got to the corner and he finally got the display case unlocked, we found calculators instead of language translators. The salesman wandered around the store trying to find the item I had requested. Finally he yelled at another employee, "Hey Joe, where are the language translators?" Finally we found them, but as you might have guessed, he knew nothing about how they worked.

After reciting similar "horror stories," employees could then be asked to describe a more appropriate response in each case. In my personal story above, a proper response would be for the two employees to cease their conversation immediately upon my entry into the store. One of them should have personally greeted me with a smile and an open ended question such as, "What can I help you find today?" He should have known where everything was located, as well as the operational characteristics. In cases where that knowledge is lacking, the customer should be referred to another employee who does have the knowledge.

Listening to Customers to Determine Needs

Quite often customers have only a vague notion of what they are looking for. They sometimes are not very articulate in describing the product. It is crucial that store personnel listen carefully to gather clues about the customer's needs. Store employees naturally "turn off" when they see customers struggling to describe their needs. Store personnel may even tell you "We do not have that item," and then a few minutes later, you would stumble across it. In such cases, the store employee was not listening attentively and not asking key questions to pinpoint the customer's needs. Again, these types of situations can be practiced by role playing during company meetings or informal gatherings.

Learning to Handle Unusual Customer Problems

Sooner or later in nearly all businesses, unusual circumstances occur that can tax the ingenuity of store personnel. For example, on the day after the high school prom a teenager brings back a cocktail dress purchased in the store a few days before, claiming that she did not like the color of the dress and wants to return it for a cash refund. What do you do?

Owners of photo studios have recounted situations where a person will bring back photos that were purchased a month before.

The person claims that he did not like the photos because they were not a flattering likeness of him. How do you handle this?

Here's a firsthand example. Several years ago, I was installing quarry tile in an entry way to our family room. I went to the tile specialty store to purchase the tile and the grouting. I asked the sales person at least twice if he was sure that this was the correct type of grouting. He assured me that it was. After I applied the grouting, it started cracking within two days. Upon closer examination, I found the grouting was for small ceramic tile such as those used on bathroom walls. It had none of the coarser sand in it that was needed to bind the material over a greater gap. When I took the remaining grouting back to the tile store and complained that they have given me the wrong grouting and that it had caused me to waste several hours of my time and had ended in an unsatisfactory job, all I got was an admittance that it was the wrong grouting; no money back, no compensation for lost time.

How would you have reacted to these problems if you had been working in the store? There are no easy answers. Each store should have general guidelines about how to handle such problems. For example in the case of the cocktail dress, the store should have had a returns policy plainly stated on signs and on receipts. Some clothing stores have signs stating that apparel may not be returned after wear except in cases where there are defects in material or workmanship. But employees should be encouraged to use common sense in dealing with these matters, always giving the benefit of the doubt to the customer. Many employees would assume that because the cocktail dress was returned after the prom, then surely it must have been worn to the prom. To me, the answer is fairly simple. If the dress shows no sign of wear, give the refund. If the dress has stains that indicate it had been worn, refer to the policy of no returns after wearing.

In the case of the photographs, policy statements need to be displayed through signs and on receipts. For example, a policy could state that unsatisfactory photographs must be returned within seven days for refund. Store employees could then point out to the customer that there has to be a limit; it is seven days, and they far exceeded the time period.

In a case where store personnel give customers erroneous information or the wrong material—such as in the case of the tile grout—the store should accept some responsibility for the outcome.

Most stores should have contingency plans of incremental offers, based on the seriousness of the situation and the disposition of the customer. For example, in the case of the cocktail dress and the photos, perhaps a first step would be to offer a credit, but no cash rebate. If the customer is adamant, perhaps the next offer would be to rebate a percent of the purchase amount, say 80%. If it appears that the customer will settle for no less than a full cash rebate, that is probably the best solution, although the owner's or manager's approval may be required.

Ultimately, store personnel should keep in mind that most customers are reasonable human beings and are not going to try to take advantage of the store. When you experience an unusual situation, it pays to keep in mind the damage to your business that an unhappy customer can cause, and take action to satisfy the customer.

When unusual situations are thought through and rehearsed before the fact, the actual event can be concluded smoothly and with as little damage to the company's reputation as possible. A parallel can be drawn with pre-thinking appropriate actions for possible emergencies that might come up. This was true in my role as an aviator in the military for several years as described below.

In the military, we continually rehearsed remedial action for possible flight emergencies. One rehearsal applied to a possible tire blow-out. During my two years in Vietnam, the rehearsals paid off several times. For example, during my second tour of duty, I was flying a twin engine turbo-prop reconnaissance aircraft. Each night around midnight, my radar operator and I would take off from our airfield near Saigon and fly along the Cambodian and Laotian borders to near North Vietnam and return. The aircraft was very heavy and we were flying off a very short rock runway. The sharp rocks in the runway would often puncture the overloaded tires and cause them to blow out. This was not a particularly dangerous situation unless it happened just before lift off. Most of the aviators in the unit believed that, in such a case, the takeoff should be aborted and full reverse pitch used to stop the airplane. However, a few believed that the airplane should be lifted off and brought back around for a landing with one flat tire. One night, I blew a tire just before lift off and I instantaneously applied full reverse thrust and brought the airplane to a stop at the end of the runway. No damage was done and a new tire quickly got us on our way. A few nights later a friend who believed that my way was the wrong way, also blew a tire just before lift off. However, according to his instincts, he lifted the aircraft off and came back around to land. Upon landing he blew all the other tires and completely wiped out the landing gear, which caused major damage to the aircraft. Rehearsal in one's mind before the fact makes the actual incident go must easier, providing you are rehearsing the proper procedures. For example, employees who think through possible returns predicaments and proper responses will probably be able to handle them in a smooth manner, should they occur.

Going the Extra Mile for the Customer

Employees should be taught to treat every customer as though she or he is the most important customer the company has. I had been asked to be a keynote speaker at a retail conference in the South Pacific a few months from now. My schedule was such that I would be speaking not too long after completing 17 hours of flying time and going through several time zones. I had hoped to buy a coach ticket for myself and use awards to upgrade it to business class so that I could be better rested upon arrival. I had called the airline on two previous nights to try to arrange this. In each case I was informed in a brusque manner that this flight is always full and it was virtually impossible to use awards for an upgrade. I was feeling pretty depressed about my primary airline treating me in such a curt manner. Today I tried one more time. My persistence paid off. My call was answered by a wonderful woman who immediately pulled up my record (I have flown over 500,000 miles on this airline and am a member of their 100,000 mile club). Her first response was, "We really appreciate customers like you, Mister Stone, let me see what I can do." I could hear the computer keys clicking as she worked diligently for several minutes on the problem, informing me of her progress from time to time. Finally she said, "I have it all worked out, Mr. Stone," and she gave me the details of the flight segments. I thanked her profusely, but her modest response was "I know how tiring those long flights can be, I just try to do what I can to make our customers' trips a little easier." As far as I am concerned, she went the extra mile for me and I got her name and intend to write a letter of commendation to her supervisor.

Some clothing store owners have a policy of letting customers take out several garments on "approval" so that they can try on the clothes in their own home under their lighting and check the colors against their accessories and get the opinions of friends and family members. Many people really appreciate this feature. This is another example of going the extra mile.

Several small businesses encourage store personnel to deliver bulky items, items purchased over the phone, or items left for repair, directly to customers' homes on their way home from work, if they live in the vicinity. For busy customers, this is a much appreciated service. Employees may be compensated with, for example, a free tank of gas.

SUMMARY OF STEPS TO QUALITY SERVICE

Owners and managers of local stores must make a strong commitment to putting together the strongest team that they can to serve the company's customers. Again, the following are important steps.

1. **Hire the Right People in the First Place.** Think through the job requirements and write a good job description. Advertise in the places where good candidates would likely take notice. Have applicants fill out a good application form. Study the forms closely and try to choose the best candidates to interview. Interview the candidates in your place of business. show them the operation and introduce them to other employees. Be sure to check

references. Try to make your decision based on overall qualifications and on your opinion of how the person will get along with customers and other employees.

2. **Train Employees Thoroughly.** Make sure that new employees are trained well initially. They should be well versed on company policies. They should be familiar with the products and services sold. They should be well trained in the operation of machines including computers and cash registers.

   Encourage reading of trade journals and consumer magazines so that employees stay abreast of industry developments. Try to take an employee or two to trade shows so that they can view the latest merchandise and concepts. In addition, the interaction with contemporaries is an important aspect of trade shows.

   Keep a video cassette recorder (VCR) around and procure tapes on products and on various job skills such as customer relations, salesmanship, telephone etiquette. Encourage employees to view the tapes during slow times.

3. **Communicate Well.** Do everything possible to make sure that everyone in the business knows what is going on in the store. A good start is to institute regular company meetings, preferably at least monthly. Employees should be told of trends in sales, new products, changes in company policy, etc. A forum should be provided to get input from employees who are on the front lines and in a good position to gauge consumer sentiments. Ask for their recommendations.

   If you have more than a few employees, consider publishing an informal weekly newsletter that reports interesting business and social happenings. Recognize people for accomplishments and congratulate them on awards, births, anniversaries, etc.

   Consider holding an annual meeting where the company's progress is analyzed. Get employees involved in helping to set goals. Reward them when goals are met.

   Conduct regular social events. There is a lot of merit in the saying that "A company that plays well together, works well together."

4. **Instill a Strong Customer Orientation.** Through role playing at company meetings and informal conversations between employees, develop a caring attitude among employees. Get them to treat each customer as though he or she were the most important person in the world.

A customer orientation begins with greeting each customer in a friendly manner and learning to listen to them to determine their needs. Encourage employees to think through all the unusual circumstances that could happen and determine a proper response. When the time comes that such a circumstance arises, unusual circumstances can be handled in a much smoother manner.

Get employees to consider how they can go the "extra mile" for their customers. This is one of the most effective methods of developing loyal customers. Customers quickly recognize companies that have well-trained employees who work together as a team, and reward them with their business.

Appendix 1

Location of Wal-Mart Stores by State

Alabama

Adamsville
Alabaster
Alexander City
Andalusia
Anniston
Arab
Athens
Attalla
Auburn
Bessemer
Birmingham
Boaz
Brent
Brewton
Clanton
Cullman
Daphne
Decatur
Demopolis
Dothan
Enterprise
Eufaula
Fairfield
Fayette
Florence
Foley
Fort Payne
Gadsden
Gardendale
Geneva
Greenville
Haleyville
Hamilton
Hartselle
Huntsville
Jacksonville
Jasper

Leeds
Livingston
Mobile
Monroeville
Montgomery
Moulton
Oneonta
Opelika
Ozark
Phenix City
Prattville
Roanoke
Russellville
Saraland
Scottsboro
Selma
Sheffield
Sylacauga
Talladega
Tallassee
Thomasville
Troy
Tuscaloosa
Valley
Wetumpka
Winfield

Arkansas

Alma
Arkadelphia
Ash Flat
Ashdown
Batesville
Benton
Bentonville
Berryville
Blytheville
Booneville

Brinkley
Camden
Clarksville
Clinton
Conway
Corning
Crossett
Dardanelle
De Queen
Dumas
El Dorado
Fayetteville
Flippin
Fordyce
Forrest City
Fort Smith
Harrison
Heber Springs
Hope
Hot Springs Natnl. Pa
Huntsville
Jacksonville
Jonesboro
Little Rock
Lonoke
Magnolia
Malvern
Mc Gehee
Mena
Monticello
Morrilton
Mountain Home
Mountain View
Nashville
Newport
North Little Rock
Osceola
Ozark
Paragould

Paris
Pine Bluff
Pocahontas
Rogers
Russellville
Searcy
Sheridan
Siloam Springs
Springdale
Stuttgart
Texarkana
Trumann
Van Buren
Waldron
Walnut Ridge
West Helena
West Memphis
Wynne

Arizona

Apache Junction
Casa Grande
Chandler
Cottonwood
Douglas
Flagstaff
Glendale
Globe
Green Valley
Lake Havasu City
Mesa
Nogales
Page
Payson
Peoria
Phoenix
Prescott
Riviera
Show Low
Sierra Vista
Tempe
Thatcher
Tucson
Winslow
Yuma

California

Bakersfield
Barstow
Calexico
Cathedral City
Colton

Corona
Crescent City
El Centro
Elk Grove
Folsom
Fontana
Fresno
Hanford
Hemet
Highland
La Quinta
Lancaster
Lodi
Los Angeles
Madera
Manteca
Mcclellan Afb
Modesto
Oroville
Palmdale
Perris
Pittsburg
Poway
Rancho Cucamonga
Red Bluff
Redlands
Rialto
Ridgecrest
Riverside
Rohnert Park
Santee
Stockton
Susanville
Vacaville
Vallejo
Victorville
Yucca Valley

Colorado

Alamosa
Aurora
Avon
Canon City
Castle Rock
Colorado Springs
Cortez
Denver
Englewood
Fort Collins
Fountain
Frisco
Glenwood Springs
Grand Junction

Greeley
Gunnison
La Junta
Lafayette
Littleton
Longmont
Loveland
Montrose
Pueblo
Salida
Sterling
Trinidad
Wheat Ridge

Connecticut

South Windsor

Delaware

Dover
Milford

Florida

Altamonte Springs
Apopka
Arcadia
Auburndale
Bartow
Bradenton
Brandon
Brooksville
Bushnell
Cape Coral
Casselberry
Chiefland
Crestview
Daytona Beach
De Funiak Springs
Deland
Delray Beach
Destin
Dunnellon
Eustis
Fernandina Beach
Fort Lauderdale
Fort Myers
Fort Pierce
Fort Walton Beach
Gainesville
Haines City
Hialeah
Hollywood

Homosassa
Inverness
Jacksonville
Jacksonville Beach
Kissimmee
Lake City
Lake Wales
Lake Worth
Lakeland
Land O Lakes
Largo
Leesburg
Macclenny
Marianna
Melbourne
Merritt Island
Miami
Milton
Mount Dora
Naples
New Port Richey
New Smyrna Beach
Ocala
Ocoee
Okeechobee
Orange City
Orange Park
Orlando
Ormond Beach
Palatka
Palm Coast
Palm Harbor
Panama City
Pensacola
Pinellas Park
Pompano Beach
Port Charlotte
Port Richey
Port Saint Lucie
Punta Gorda
Quincy
Rockledge
Saint Augustine
Saint Cloud
Saint Petersburg
Sanford
Sarasota
Sebastian
Sebring
Seffner
Spring Hill
Stuart
Sun City Center
Tallahassee
Tampa

Titusville
Venice
Vero Beach
Wauchula
West Palm Beach
Winter Haven
Zephyrhills

Georgia

Albany
Americus
Athens
Augusta
Austell
Bremen
Brunswick
Buford
Cairo
Calhoun
Camilla
Canton
Carrollton
Cartersville
Cedartown
Columbus
Commerce
Cordele
Cornelia
Covington
Cumming
Dallas
Dalton
Decatur
Douglas
Douglasville
Dublin
Eastman
Elberton
Ellijay
Fayetteville
Fitzgerald
Forsyth
Fort Oglethorpe
Gainesville
Griffin
Hartwell
Hazlehurst
Hinesville
Kennesaw
La Grange
Lawrenceville
Lilburn
Macon

Madison
Marietta
Milledgeville
Monroe
Morrow
Moultrie
Newnan
Rincon
Riverdale
Rome
Roswell
Saint Marys
Sandersville
Savannah
Snellville
Statesboro
Stockbridge
Stone Mountain
Summerville
Surrency
Swainsboro
Thomaston
Thomasville
Thomson
Tifton
Toccoa
Union City
Valdosta
Vidalia
Warner Robins
Waycross
Winder
Woodstock

Iowa

Ames
Anamosa
Ankeny
Boone
Burlington
Carroll
Cedar Falls
Cedar Rapids
Centerville
Creston
Davenport
Decorah
Denison
Des Moines
Fairfield
Fort Dodge
Grinnell
Indianola

Iowa City
Iowa Falls
Keokuk
Le Mars
Manchester
Maquoketa
Marshalltown
Mason City
Muscatine
Newton
Oskaloosa
Ottumwa
Pella
Shenandoah
Sioux Center
Sioux City
Spirit Lake
Storm Lake
Tipton
Washington
Waterloo
Waverly

Idaho

Blackfoot
Burley
Idaho Falls
Moscow
Rexburg

Illinois

Aledo
Anna
Aurora
Bardstown
Belleville
Benton
Bloomingdale
Bloomington
Bolingbrook
Bradley
Canton
Carbondale
Carlinville
Carlyle
Carmi
Centralia
Champaign
Charleston
Chester
Chicago
Clinton

Collinsville
Crystal Lake
DeKalb
Decatur
Du Quoin
Dundee
East Peoria
East Saint Louis
Edwardsville
Effingham
Elgin
Fairfield
Flora
Freeport
Galesburg
Geneseo
Granite City
Harrisburg
Harvard
Herrin
Highland
Jacksonville
Jerseyville
Joliet
Kankakee
Kewanee
La Grange
Lake Zurich
Lawrenceville
Lincoln
Litchfield
Macomb
Marion
Marshall
Marshall
Matteson
Mattoon
McHenry
Morris
Mount Prospect
Mount Vernon
Mundelein
Murphysboro
Naperville
O Fallon
Olney
Orland Park
Ottawa
Pana
Pekin
Peoria
Peru
Pittsfield
Plano
Pontiac

Princeton
Quincy
Rantoul
Robinson
Rochelle
Rock Falls
Rockford
Round Lake
Saint Charles
Salem
Sparta
Springfield
Sterling
Streamwood
Summit Argo
Taylorville
Vandalia
Washington
Waterloo
Watseka
Wheeling
Wood River

Indiana

Anderson
Angola
Auburn
Aurora
Bedford
Boonville
Brazil
Carmel
Clarksville
Clinton
Columbia City
Columbus
Connersville
Corydon
Crawfordsville
Decatur
Elkhart
Evansville
Fishers
Fort Wayne
Frankfort
Franklin
Goshen
Greencastle
Greenfield
Greensburg
Hobart
Indianapolis
Jasper

Kendallville
Lafayette
Lebanon
Linton
Logansport
Madison
Marion
Martinsville
Michigan City
Muncie
New Castle
Noblesville
North Vernon
Plainfield
Princeton
Richmond
Rochester
Rushville
Schererville
Scottsburg
Seymour
Shelbyville
Spencer
Sulllvan
Tell City
Terre Haute
Valparaiso
Vincennes
Wabash
Warsaw
Washington
Winchester

Kansas

Arkansas City
Atchison
Augusta
Baxter Springs
Bonner Springs
Chanute
Coffeyville
Colby
Concordia
Derby
Dodge City
El Dorado
Emporia
Fort Scott
Garden City
Great Bend
Hays
Hiawatha
Holton

Hutchinson
Junction City
Kansas City
Lawrence
Leavenworth
Liberal
Manhattan
Marysville
Mc Pherson
Olathe
Ottawa
Paola
Parsons
Pittsburg
Pratt
Salina
Shawnee Mlssion
Wellington
Wichita
Winfield

Kentucky

Alexandria
Ashland
Barbourville
Bardstown
Beaver Dam
Benton
Berea
Bowling Green
Campbellsville
Central City
Columbia
Corbin
Crestwood
Cynthiana
Danville
Elizabethtown
Florence
Frankfort
Franklin
Fulton
Georgetown
Glasgow
Hardinsburg
Harlan
Harrodsburg
Hazard
Henderson
Hopkinsville
Jackson
LaGrange
Lawrenceburg

Lebanon
Leitchfield
London
Louisville
Madisonville
Manchester
Mayfield
Maysville
Middlesboro
Monticello
Morehead
Morganfield
Mount Sterling
Murray
Nicholasville
Owensboro
Paducah
Paintsville
Paris
Pikeville
Prestonsburg
Princeton
Radcliff
Richmond
Russellville
Shelbyville
Somerset
Stanford
Stanford
Whitesburg
Williamsburg
Willlamstown
Winchester

Louisiana

Abbeville
Alexandria
Baker
Bastrop
Baton Rouge
Bogalusa
Breaux Bridge
Bunkie
Chalmette
Covington
Crowley
Donham Springs
Deridder
Donaldsonville
Eunice
Farmerville
Ferriday
Franklin

Galliano
Gonzales
Gretna
Hammond
Harvey
Haughton
Homer
Houma
Jena
Jennings
Jonesboro
Kenner
LaPlace
Lafayette
Lake Charles
Leesville
Lockport
Mansfield
Many
Marksville
Metairie
Minden
Monroe
Morgan City
Natchitoches
New Iberia
New Orleans
New Roads
Oak Grove
Oakdale
Opelousas
Pineville
Plaquemine
Port Allen
Rayville
Ruston
Saint Martinville
Shreveport
Slidell
Springhill
Sulphur
Thibodaux
Ville Platte
Vivian
West Monroe
Winnfield
Winnsboro
Zachary

Massachusetts

Bellingham
Fairhaven

Maryland

Aberdeen
Easton
Elkton
Glen Burnie
Hagerstown
Prince Frederick
Salisbury
Waldorf
Westminster

Maine

Auburn
Bangor
Brunswick
Lincoln
Rockland
Sanford
Scarborough

Michigan

Adrian
Alma
Bay City
Big Rapids
Cadillac
Caro
Charlotte
Coldwater
Flint
Fremont
Gaylord
Holland
Howell
Jonesville
Monroe
Mount Pleasant
Owosso
Saint Johns
Sault Sainte Marie
South Haven
Sturgis
Ypsilanti

Minnesota

Albert Lea
Alexandria
Blue Earth
Brainerd
Buffalo

Cloquet
Dilworth
Duluth
Eden Prairie
Faribault
Fergus Falls
Grand Rapids
Hastings
Hutchinson
Little Falls
Mankato
Marshall
Minneapolis
Montevideo
Owatonna
Redwood Falls
Rochester
Saint Cloud
Saint Paul
Stillwater
Waseca
Willmar

Missouri

Arnold
Aurora
Ava
Belton
Bethany
Blue Springs
Bolivar
Boonville
Branson
Buffalo
Butler
Camdenton
Cameron
Cape Girardeau
Carthage
Caruthersville
Cassville
Chillicothe
Clinton
Columbia
Cuba
De Soto
Dexter
Eldon
Eureka
Excelsior Springs
Farmington
Fenton
Festus

Flat River
Fulton
Hannibal
Harrisonville
Higginsville
High Ridge
Houston
Independence
Jackson
Jefferson City
Joplin
Kansas City
Kennett
Kirksville
Lamar
Lebanon
Lees Summit
Liberty
Louisiana
Macon
Marshall
Marshfield
Maryville
Mexico
Monett
Mountain Grove
Mountain View
Neosho
Nevada
Osage Beach
Owensville
Ozark
Pacific
Perryville
Piedmont
Poplar Bluff
Potosi
Republic
Richmond
Rolla
Saint Ann
Saint Charles
Saint Joseph
Saint Louis
Salem
Savannah
Sedalia
Sikeston
Springfield
Sullivan
Thayer
Troy
Union
Versailles
Warrensburg

Warrenton
Warsaw
Washington
Waynesville
Webb City
Wentzville
West Plains

Mississippi

Aberdeen
Amory
Avalon
Batesville
Biloxi
Booneville
Brandon
Brookhaven
Carthage
Clarksdale
Cleveland
Clinton
Columbia
Columbus
Corinth
Forest
Fulton
Greenville
Greenwood
Grenada
Gulfport
Hattiesburg
Hazlehurst
Holly Springs
Houston
Indianola
Iuka
Jackson
Kosciusko
Laurel
Louisville
Lucedale
Magee
McComb
Meridian
Natchez
New Albany
Ocean Springs
Oxford
Pascagoula
Petal
Philadelphia
Picayune
Pontotoc

Ridgeland
Ripley
Senatobia
Southaven
Starkville
Tupelo
Vicksburg
Waveland
West
West Point
Winona

Montana

Butte
Helena

North Carolina

Ahoskie
Albermarle
Asheboro
Asheville
Burlington
Clyde
Concord
Dunn
Durham
Eden
Elizabeth City
Elizabethtown
Elkin
Fayetteville
Franklin
Garner
Gastonia
Goldsboro
Greensboro
Greenville
Hendersonville
Hickory
High Point
Hillsborough
Jacksonville
Kinston
Kitty Hawk
Knightdale
Laurinburg
Lenoir
Lexington
Lincolnton
Louisburg
Lumberton
Marion

Mocksville
Monroe
Mooresville
Morehead City
Morganton
Mount Airy
Murphy
New Bern
Oxford
Pisgah Forest
Raleigh
Roanoke Rapids
Rockingham
Rocky Mount
Roxboro
Rural Hall
Rutherfordton
Salisbury
Sanford
Shallotte
Shelby
Smithfield
Southern Pines
Spindale
Spring Lake
Statesville
Taylorsville
Wadesboro
Wallace
Washington
Waynesville
Whiteville
Wilkesboro
Wilmington

North Dakota

Bismarck
Devils Lake
Dickinson
Fargo
Grand Forks
Jamestown
Minot
Williston

Nebraska

Columbus
Fairbury
Fremont
Grand Island
Hastings
Kearney

McCook
Norfolk
North Platte
Omaha
Scottsbluff
Seward
South Sioux City
York

New Hampshire

Amherst
Derry
Hooksett
Hudson
Plaistow
Seabrook
Somersworth

New Jersey

Berlin
Blackwood
Brick
Manahawkin
Toms River

New Mexico

Alamogordo
Albuquerque
Belen
Carlsbad
Clovis
Fannington
Gallup
Hobbs
Las Cruces
Las Vegas
Roswell
Ruidoso
Santa Fe
Silver City
Taos

Nevada

Carson City
Las Vegas

New York

Auburn
Canandaigua

Cortland
East Greenbush
Geneseo
Geneva
Gloversville
Liverpool
Newark
Niagra Falls
Oswego
Rochester
Seneca Falls
Vestal
Watertown
Webster

Ohio

Ashland
Bellefontaine
Celina
Cincinnati
Circleville
Coshocton
Dayton
East Liverpool
Elyria
Findlay
Fremont
Jackson
Lebanon
Lima
Mansfield
Marion
Marysville
Medina
Mentor
Miamisburg
Millersburg
Napoleon
Newark
Pataskala
Port Clinton
Portsmouth
Sandusky
Sidney
South Point
Tiffin
Troy
Urbana
Van Wert
West Union
Willoughby
Wilmington
Wooster
Xenia

Oklahoma

Ada
Altus
Alva
Anadarko
Ardmore
Atoka
Bartlesville
Blackwell
Bristow
Broken Arrow
Broken Bow
Chandler
Checotah
Chickasha
Claremore
Cleveland
Coweta
Cushing
Duncan
Durant
Edmond
El Reno
Elk City
Enid
Grove
Guthrie
Guymon
Henryetta
Holdenville
Hugo
Idabel
Jay
Jenks
Kingfisher
Lawton
Lindsay
Madill
Marlow
Mcalester
Miami
Muskogee
Mustang
Newcastle
Norman
Nowata
Oklahoma City
Okmulgee
Owasso
Pauls Valley
Pawhuska
Ponca City
Poteau
Pryor
Purcell
Sallisaw
Sand Springs
Sapulpa
Seminole
Skiatook
Stigler
Stillwater
Stilwell
Sulphur
Tahlequah
Tulsa
Vinita
Wagoner
Weatherford
Woodward
Yukon

Oregon

Coos Bay
Grants Pass
Hemiston
Hood Rlver
Klamath Falls
La Grande
Lebanon
Mcminnville
Newport
Ontario
Salem
Woodburn

Pennsylvania

Bloomsburg
Butler
Chambersburg
Du Bois
Everett
Gettysburg
Hanover
Harrisburg
Hermitage
Kittanning
Lewisburg
Lewistown
Mars
Meadville
Mechanicsburg
Monaca
Montoursville
New Cumberland
Olyphant
Reading
Saint Marys
Somerset
State College
Wilkes Barre
York

South Carolina

Aiken
Anderson
Barnwell
Beaufort
Camden
Charleston
Cheraw
Chester
Clemson
Columbia
Conway
Dillon
Easley
Florence
Gaffney
Georgetown
Greenville
Hartsville
Hilton Head Island
Lake City
Lancaster
Laurens
Lexington
Marion
Moncks Corner
Mount Pleasant
Myrtle Beach
Newberry
North Augusta
Orangeburg
Rock Hill
Seneca
Spartanburg
Summerville
Sumter
Taylors
Union
Walterboro
West Columbia
York

South Dakota

Aberdeen

Brookings
Pierre
Rapid City
Sioux Falls
Spearfish
Watertown
Yankton

Tennessee

Ashland City
Athens
Bolivar
Bristol
Brownsville
Camden
Camden
Carthage
Chattanooga
Clarksville
Cleveland
Collierville
Columbia
Cookeville
Covington
Crossville
Dayton
Dickson
Dyersburg
Elizabethton
Fayetteville
Franklin
Gallatin
Greeneville
Hendersonville
Hermitage
Hixson
Hohenwald
Humboldt
Huntingdon
Jackson
Jamestown
Jefferson City
Johnson City
Kingsport
Knoxville
La Follette
Lafayette
Lawrenceburg
Lebanon
Lenoir City
Lewisburg
Lexington
Madison

Madisonville
Manchester
Maryville
McKenzie
McMlnnville
Memphis
Milan
Millington
Morristown
Murfreesboro
Nashville
Newport
Oak Ridge
Oneida
Paris
Powell
Pulaski
Ripley
Rockwood
Savannah
Selmer
Sevierville
Shelbyville
Smyrna
Soddy Daisy
South Pittsburg
Sparta
Springfield
Tullahoma
Union City
Waverly
Winchester

Texas

Abilene
Alice
Alief
Allen
Alvin
Amarillo
Angleton
Aransas Pass
Athens
Atlanta
Austin
Ballinger
Bastrop
Bay City
Baytown
Beaumont
Bedford
Beeville
Belton

Big Spring
Boerne
Bonham
Borger
Bowie
Brady
Breckenridge
Brenham
Bridge City
Brownsville
Brownwood
Bryan
Burkburnett
Burleson
Caldwell
Canton
Canyon
Carrizo Springs
Carrollton
Carthage
Center
Childress
Clarksville
Cleburne
Cleveland
College Station
Columbus
Commerce
Conroe
Copperas Cove
Corpus Christi
Corsicana
Crockett
Crosby
Cuero
Dallas
Decatur
Del Rio
Denison
Denton
Dumas
Duncanville
Eagle Pass
Eastland
Edinburg
Edna
El Campo
El Paso
Ennis
Falfurrias
Floresville
Fort Stockton
Fort Worth
Fredericksburg
Gainesville

Galveston
Garland
Gatesville
Georgetown
Giddings
Gilmer
Gonzales
Graham
Granbury
Grand Prairie
Greenville
Groves
Hallettsville
Harlingen
Hempstead
Henderson
Hillsboro
Hitchcock
Hondo
Houston
Humble
Huntsville
Iowa Park
Irving
Jacksonville
Jasper
Katy
Kenedy
Kerrville
Kilgore
Killeen
Kingsville
La Grange
Lake Jackson
Lamesa
Lampasas
Laredo
Levelland
Lewisville
Liberty
Livingston
Lockhart
Longview
Lubbock
Lubbock
Lufkin
Lumberton
Mabank
Madisonville
Mansfield
Marble Falls
Marlin
Marshall
McKinney
Mcallen

Mesquite
Mexia
Midland
Mineola
Mineral Wells
Mission
Mount Pleasant
Nacogdoches
Navasota
Nederland
New Boston
New Braunfels
Odessa
Orange
Palestine
Pampa
Paris
Pasadena
Pearland
Pearsall
Pecos
Plainview
Plano
Pleasanton
Port Isabel
Port Lavaca
Porter
Raymondville
Rockdale
Rockport
Rockwall
Rosenberg
Round Rock
San Angelo
San Antonio
San Benito
San Marcos
Sealy
Seguin
Seminole
Sherman
Sherman
Silsbee
Snyder
Spring
Stafford
Stamford
Stephenviile
Sulphur Springs
Taylor
Temple
Terrell
Tomball
Tyler
Uvalde

Victoria
Vidor
Waco
Waxahachie
Weatherford
Webster
Weslaco
West Columbia
Wichita Falls
Woodville

Utah

Cedar City
Layton
Logan
Ogden
Orem
Park City
Price
Salt Lake City
St George
Tooele
Vernal

Virginia

Bodford
Big Stone Gap
Bluefield
Charlottesville
Chesapeake
Christiansburg
Colonial Heights
Danville
Farrnville
Fredericksburg
Galax
Glen Allen
Gloucester
Hampton
Harrisonburg
Lexington
Lynchburg
Manassas
Marion
Martinsville
Mechanicsville
Newport News
Norfolk
Norton
Portsmouth
Pulaski
Roanoke

Salem
South Boston
South Hill
Staunton
Suffolk
Tappahannock
Virginia Beach
Winchester

West Virginia

Beckley
Bluefield
Clarksburg
Elkins
Fairmont
Martinsburg
Oak Hill
Ripley
Summersville
Vienna
Weston

Wisconsin

Appleton
Ashland
Baraboo

Beaver Dam
Berlin
Black River Falls
Delafield
Dodgeville
Eau Claire
Fond Du Lac
Green Bay
Hudson
Janesville
Kenosha
Lake Geneva
Madison
Manitowoc
Menomonee Falls
Menomonie
Merrill
Milwaukee
Monroe
Mukwonago
New London
Oak Creek
Onalaska
Oshkosh
Platteville
Portage
Prairie Du Chien
Rhinelander

Rice Lake
Richland Center
Saulville
Sheboygan
Sparta
Stevens Point
Stoughton
Sturgeon Bay
Sun Prairie
Superior
Tomah
Viroqua
Watertown
Waukesha
Whitewater
Wisconsin Rapids

Wyoming

Casper
Cheyenne
Cody
Evanston
Gillette
Laramie
Rock Springs
Sheridan

Appendix 2

Location of
Home Depot Stores
By State

City	State	Zip	Address
Mobile	AL	36609	851 Montlimar Dr
Mesa	AZ	85205	
Mesa	AZ	85210	1300 S Country Club Dr
Peoria	AZ	85382	6880 W Bell Rd
Phoenix	AZ	85022	12434 N Cave Creek Rd
Phoenix	AZ	85019	4240 W Camelback Rd
Phoenix	AZ	85035	7333 W Mcdowell Rd
Phoenix	AZ	85016	3130 E Thomas Rd
Scottsdale	AZ	85250	9170 E Indian Bend Rd
Tempe	AZ	85284	725 W Warner Rd
Tucson	AZ	85710	7102 E Broadway Blvd
Tucson	AZ	85705	4755 N Oracle Rd
Anaheim	CA	92801	2300 W Lincoln Ave
Campbell	CA	95008	480 E Hamilton Ave
Canoga Park	CA	91304	21218 Roscoe Blvd
Carmichael	CA	95608	6001 Madison Ave
Cerritos	CA	90701	10930 Alondra Blvd
Chino	CA	91710	5450 Walnut Ave
Chula Vista	CA	91910	390 E H St
Chula Vista	CA	91913	525 Sauterne Pl
Concord	CA	94520	2090 Meridian Park Blvd
Corona	CA	91719	490 N Mckinley St
Covina	CA	91722	1348 N Azusa Ave
Daly City	CA	94014	91 Colma Blvd
El Cajon	CA	92020	965 Arnele Ave
Escondido	CA	92029	1352 W Valley Pky
Fairfield	CA	94533	2121 Cadenasso Dr
Fullerton	CA	92631	601 S Placentia Ave
Gardena	CA	90248	18233 S Hoover St

City	State	Zip	Address
Glendale	CA	91204	5040 San Fernando Rd
Hawthorne	CA	90250	14603 Ocean Gate Ave
Huntington Beach	CA	92647	6912 Edinger Ave
La Mirada	CA	90638	12300 La Mirada Blvd
La Puente	CA	91748	18131 Gale Ave
Long Beach	CA	90806	2450 Cherry Ave
Long Beach	CA	90807	4550 Atlantic Ave
Milpitas	CA	95035	1535 Landess Ave
Monrovia	CA	91016	407 W Huntington Dr
Newbury Park	CA	91320	500 N Ventu Park Rd
Oceanside	CA	92056	3838 Vista Way
Orange	CA	92667	435 W Katelia Ave
Oxnard	CA	93030	2600 E Vineyard Ave
Palmdale	CA	93551	340 W Aven #-P
Pico Rivera	CA	90660	9200 Whittier Blvd
Pleasanton	CA	94588	6000 Johnson Dr
Rohnert Park	CA	94928	4825 Redwood Dr
Sacramento	CA	95823	4641 Florin Rd
San Bernardino	CA	92408	695 E Hospitality Ln
San Bernardino	CA	92405	1055 W 21st St
San Carlos	CA	94070	1125 Old County Rd
San Diego	CA	92111	7803 Othello Ave
San Diego	CA	92128	12185 Carmel Mountain Rd
San Diego	CA	92117	4255 Genesee Ave
San Diego	CA	92115	6611 UniversityAve
San Diego	CA	92110	3555 Sports Arena Blvd
San Leandro	CA	94577	1933 Davis St
Santa Ana	CA	92704	3500 W Macarthur Blvd
Santa Clara	CA	95050	2435 Lafayette St
Santee	CA	92071	255 Town Center Pky
Sylmar	CA	91342	12960 Foothill Blvd
Tustin	CA	92680	2782 El Camino Real
Union City	CA	94587	30055 Industrial Pky
Upland	CA	91786	250 S Mountain Ave
Vallejo	CA	94591	1175 Admiral Callaghan Ln
Van Nuys	CA	91406	16810 Roscoe Blvd
Westminster	CA	92683	6633 Westminster Bivd
Danbury	CT	06811	114 Federal Rd
Fairfield	CT	06430	541 Kings High
Kensington	CT	06037	225 Wilbur Cross Hwy
Manchester	CT	06040	80 Buckland Hills Dr
North Haven	CT	06473	111 Universal Dr N
Norwalk	CT	06851	54 King St
Orange	CT	06477	440 Boston Post Rd
Southington	CT	06489	713 Oueen St
Stamford	CT	06902	541 Kings Hwy
Stamford	CT	06902	541 Kings Hwy

City	State	Zip	Address
Stamford	CT	06902	541 Kings Hwy
Stamford	CT	06902	541 Kings Hwy
Altamonte Springs	FL	32714	882 W State Road 436
Boca Raton	FL	33434	9820 Glades Rd
Boynton Beach	FL	33426	1500 SW 8th St
Bradenton	FL	34207	2350 Cortez Rd W
Clearwater	FL	34625	21870 US Highway 19n N
Clearwater	FL	34621	30144 US Highway 19n N
Daytona Beach	FL	32114	2455 Volusia Ave
Deerfield Beach	FL	33442	60 Sw 12th Ave
Fort Lauderdale	FL	33313	6101 NW 31st St
Fort Lauderdale	FL	33313	3001 N State Road 7
Fort Lauderdale	FL	33324	2300 S University Dr
Fort Myers	FL	33907	13300 S Cleveland Ave
Fort Myers	FL	33919	6325 Presidential Ct
Gainesville	FL	32607	7107 NW 4th Blvd
Hialeah	FL	33014	5500 NW 167th St
Hialeah	FL	33012	1700 W 49th St
Hollywood	FL	33023	1951 S State Road 7
Jacksonville	FL	32244	8151 Blanding Blvd
Jacksonville	FL	32256	9021 Southside Blvd
Jacksonville	FL	32205	5800 Ramona Blvd
Jacksonville	FL	32225	9355 Atlantic Blvd
Lake Worth	FL	33461	4241 Lake Worth Rd
Largo	FL	34641	10475 Ulmerton Rd
Longwood	FL	32750	3455 N US Highway 17 #-92
Melbourne	FL	32904	2865 W New Haven Ave
Miami	FL	33165	11305 SW 40th St
Miami	FL	33157	16051 S Dixie Hwy
Miami	FL	33144	7797 W Flagler St
Miami	FL	33186	12700 N Kendall Dr
Miami	FL	33179	1650 Ne Miami Gardens Dr
Naples	FL	33942	2251 Pine Ridge Rd
Orlando	FL	32807	6130 E Colonial Dr
Orlando	FL	32818	7022 W Colonial Dr
Orlando	FL	32809	7423 Southland Blvd
Pompano Beach	FL	33064	1151 NW 24th St
Port Charlotte	FL	33948	1800 Tamiami Trl
Port Richey	FL	34668	10017 US Highway 19
Saint Petersburg	FL	33713	1725 34th St N
Sarasota	FL	34233	4088 Cattlemen Rd
Stuart	FL	34997	3451 N Federal Hwy
Tampa	FL	33618	16121 N Dale Mabry Hwy
Tampa	FL	33604	8330 N Florida Ave
Tampa	FL	33614	3908 W Hillsborough Ave
Tampa	FL	33619	10011 Adarno Dr
Tampa	FL	33619	9941 Adamo Dr

City	State	Zip	Address
West Palm Beach	FL	33403	3860 Northlake Blvd
West Palm Beach	FL	33411	160 State Road 7 N
Atlanta	GA	30339	3905 Cumberland Pky NW
Atlanta	GA	30354	3850 Jonesboro Rd Se
Atlanta	GA	30305	2755 Piedmont Rd Ne
Atlanta	GA	30360	4343 Tilly Mill Rd
Atlanta	GA	30339	2727 Paces Ferry Rd
Austell	GA	30001	3999 Austell Rd
Decatur	GA	30035	4325 New Snapfinger Woods Dr
Decatur	GA	30032	4380 Memorial Dr
Douglasville	GA	30135	7400 Douglas Blvd
Duluth	GA	30136	3755 Shackleford Rd
Kennesaw	GA	30144	449 Roberts Ct
Lilburn	GA	30247	4121 Highway 78 SW
Marietta	GA	30067	1901 Terrell Mill Rd
Marietta	GA	30062	4101 Roswell Rd
Morrow	GA	30260	2034 Mount Zion Rd
Roswell	GA	30076	1425 Market Blvd
Woodstock	GA	30188	7120 E Alabama Rd
Baton Rouge	LA	70815	9618 Airline Hwy
Gretna	LA	70053	62 Westbank Expy
Kenner	LA	70062	2625 Veterans Memorial Blvd
New Orleans	LA	70123	1000 S Clearview Pky
New Orleans	LA	70128	12300 I 10 Service Rd
Shreveport	LA	71105	110 E Bert Kouns Industrial L
Shreveport	LA	71108	2705 W 70th St
Attleboro	MA	02703	1270 Newport Ave
Danvers	MA	01923	82 Newbury St
Quincy	MA	02169	177 Willard St
West Springfield	MA	01089	179 Daggett Dr
Baltimore	MD	21234	1971 E Joppa Rd
Gaithersburg	MD	20877	15740 Shady Grove Rd
Glen Burnie	MD	21060	601 E Ordnance Rd
Nashua	NH	03060	288 Daniel Webster Hwy
Salem	NH	03079	289 S Broadway
Clifton	NJ	07012	955 Bloomfield Ave
East Hanover	NJ	07936	902 Murray Rd
Eatontown	NJ	07724	310 State Hwy 36
Lakewood	NJ	08701	1900 Shorrock
Old Bridge	NJ	08857	1007 Us Highway 9
Paramus	NJ	07652	520 State Rt 17 N
South Plainfield	NJ	07080	3100 Hamilton Blvd
Succasunna	NJ	07876	281 State Route 10 E
Las Vegas	NV	89119	1030 W Sunset Rd
Las Vegas	NV	89128	861 S Rainbow Blvd
Reno	NV	89502	

City	State	Zip	Address
Bay Shore	NY	11706	1881 Sunrise Hwy
Commack	NY	11725	5025 Jericho Tpke
East Meadow	NY	11554	2000 Hempstead Tpke
Farmingdale	NY	11735	100 Wilow Park Ct
Floral Park	NY	11003	600 Hempstead Tpke
Freeport	NY	11520	160 E Sunrise Hwy
Patchogue	NY	11772	95 E Sunrise Hwy
Selden	NY	11784	401 Independence Plz
Oklahoma City	OK	73112	3040 NW 59th St
Oklahoma City	OK	73149	7400 S Shields Blvd
Warwick	RI	02886	80 Universal Blvd
Charleston	SC	29406	7554 Northwoods Blvd
Greenville	SC	29607	1118 Woodruff Rd
Spartanburg	SC	29301	1450 W O Ezell Blvd
Antioch	TN	37013	1155 Bell Rd
Brentwood	TN	37027	8101 Moores Ln
Chattanooga	TN	37421	6241Perimeter Dr
Knoxville	TN	37922	9361 Kingston Pike
Knoxville	TN	37917	4710 Centerline Dr
Nashville	TN	37206	1584 Gallatin Rd
Nashville	TN	37221	7665 Highway 70 S
Arlington	TX	76017	4611 S Cooper St
Austin	TX	78745	5400 Brodie Ln
Austin	TX	78759	10107 Research Blvd
Bedford	TX	76021	251 N Industrial Blvd
Carrollton	TX	75006	1441 W Trinity Mills Rd
Dallas	TX	75224	1975 W N W High
Dallas	TX	75237	7401 S Westmoreland Rd
Dallas	Tx	75243	8050 Forest Ln
Fort Worth	TX	76180	7601 Grapevine Hwy
Fort Worth	TX	76180	6501 NE Loop #-820
Fort Worth	TX	76109	4850 SW Loop #-820
Fort Worth	TX	76108	1650 S Cherry Ln
Houston	TX	77036	7110 Bellerive Dr
Houston	TX	77034	12336 Gull Fwy
Houston	TX	77043	1100 Lumpkin Rd
Houston	TX	77088	7703 Veterans Memorial Dr
Houston	TX	77015	13400 Market Stre
Mesquite	TX	75150	1330 N Town East Blvd
Plano	TX	75074	1224 N Central Expy
Plano	TX	75023	1801 W Parker Rd
Richardson	TX	75081	1332 S Plano Rd
San Antonio	TX	78239	4909 Windsor Hl
San Antonio	TX	78232	1066 Central Pky S
San Antonio	TX	78229	5101 Cambray Dr
Sugar Land	TX	77478	15505 Southwest Fwy